WHERE THE OCEAN MEETS THE SKY

CRISPIN LATYMER

WHERE THE OCEAN MEETS THE SKY

ADLARD COLES NAUTICAL
LONDON

This edition published by Adlard Coles Nautical
an imprint of A & C Black Publishers Ltd
36 Soho Square, London W1D 3QY
www.adlardcoles.com

Extract from 'Little Gidding', from *Four Quartets* by T S Eliot
reproduced by permission of Faber and Faber Ltd

ISBN 978-1-4081-1402-5

A CIP catalogue record for this book is available from the
British Library.

This book is produced using paper that is made from wood
grown in managed, sustainable forests. It is natural, renewable
and recyclable. The logging and manufacturing processes
conform to the environmental regulations of the country
of origin.

Typeset in 11/13 pt Sabon by Palimpsest Book Production
Limited, Grangemouth, Stirlingshire

Printed and bound in [Country] by [Printer name]

TO A MAN I NEVER KNEW
– BUT WHO MIGHT HAVE
UNDERSTOOD

CONTENTS

PROLOGUE

The Meltemi had been blowing hard from the northern Aegean throughout the night and the sea had become much more aggressive since dawn. *Pamara*, our 79ft twin diesel cruiser, was coping but being narrow-beamed had started to roll uncomfortably. Throughout the night my father had helmed from the shelter of the pilot house and after a perfunctory breakfast he sent my sister and me back down below. Aged eight and six neither of us were old enough to appreciate the conditions or possible risks as we sat crossed legged on our mother's bunk staring out of the porthole. To the lurching rhythm of the breaking waves we watched, with childlike innocence and fascination, as one minute we were astronauts looking up at the deep blue of limitless space before, rolling heavily, we became under-water explorers staring straight down into the dark green of the ocean depths searching for whales and giant squid. I remember that particular storm well. By the next morning, it had swept overboard the metal railings and dining table that were bolted to the aft-deck.

I also remember, probably assisted by photographs, my father's dominating presence at the helm.

I never had much of a relationship with my father, Hugo Latymer. He did not understand personal relationships. To do that, you need a natural interest in other people. For whatever reason, he had no interest or ability for that. I remember him as a mix of enviable physical achievements allied to a complete emotional vacuum. By the time I was old enough to be sufficiently interested to look at what relationship I did have he was an accomplished yachtsman, a recognised international botanist (a hobby he subsequently turned into a successful commercial business in Majorca) and a keen ornithologist. He had also rowed for Eton, been awarded a scholarship to Oxford, won the 'Belt of Honour' at Sandhurst as a young Grenadier officer, come 5th with my Godfather in the Monte Carlo Rally, was a member of the Royal Yacht Squadron, come second in the Baron Oetzen Cup on the Cresta (during which he co-founded the Shuttlecock Club for those who had crashed off the course more than 5 times at the infamous Shuttlecock Corner), been the youngest ever Partner at Robert Fleming and held nine City directorships including Save & Prosper where he had been one of the founding directors. The only blot to this otherwise impressive list of personal achievements was his separation from my mother in 1962 shortly after his recovery from meningitis. He may not have seen it as such but, either way, it was an impressive CV for someone who at the time of his leaving his wife, family, job and England was only 36 years old.

To top it all, various aunts and related females always described him rather too breathlessly and in blushing terms as the most handsome man they had ever seen. I was somewhat amused, therefore, to meet someone recently who knew him slightly in the early 1960s and who provided some counter balance to this litany of personal achievements by describing him more bluntly (before knowing he was my father) as 'that vain poof'.

A year later in 1963, having commissioned a 39ft 'Miller-Fifer' from Jimmy Miller and his uncle William in St Monace on the Firth of Forth, he set out to sail from England to Australia with my 20 year old future step-mother and he left our lives semi-permanently. This was a journey very few were undertaking and some years before Chichester, Rose and Knox-Johnston hit the headlines. For that much he was an unusual man, not interested in the social games of Shire England and City life. In his memoirs he wrote:

'It has seemed an easy explanation for me to account for my decision to leave the City as being due to a wish to spit out the spoon and use one's own teeth, to achieve a personal triumph rather than one engineered and supported by my father. I had an independent and slightly misanthropic attitude to the world that made me want to get out of the City, London and the Establishment and to do something wild and silly in reaction to conventional curbs.'

The downside for me was that I was only 7 when he left my life and instantly sailing became a memory. It was to be another 30 years before I realised quite how deeply that sense of freedom and the raw excitement of open water must have been ingrained in me. In 1993 I bought my first boat (a 15ft gaff rigged Cornish Shrimper) and, with impeccable timing and history repeating itself almost exactly, my own 15 year marriage irretrievably broke down six months later – coincidentally not long after my first wife had also recovered from meningitis. However, sailing gave me the escape I needed from her passion for hunting. Even now, I still flinch when I see a saddle. My mother later remarked that she knew our marriage was in trouble when I bought that boat. Perhaps it was a catalyst. All I can say with certainty and sadness is that I felt as if I was on my way to a mysterious date each time I drove to Chichester marina and set off solo into the Solent. I hadn't felt like that for a long time.

It was not totally surprising, therefore, when 44 years later I found myself facing almost identical conditions to that gale of 1961. It had to happen sooner or later. Shaunagh (my second wife), Harry (stepson), Rosie (daughter) and I were at the end of a two week cruise to northern Sardinia and southern Corsica. This time we were in my 41ft Beneteau sloop, *Fathom*. With four days before we were due to fly back to London (from Girona in Spain) we found ourselves confined to port in Sardinia by a north-westerly tramuntana. For 36 hours we sat it out before we ran out of time. Like my father, I was confident about handling bad conditions and was more concerned about how the others would feel and react. That morning the forecast pinned to the open door of the old boat-house that doubled as the local yacht club finally predicted wind speeds to drop below 30 knots later that afternoon for the first time in two days. I knew we had to leave to stand any chance of reaching Spain in time to get our return flights. Under a leaden sky the sea had been dull grey for the last 24 hours and now, through the narrow rock-strewn passage between the islands, I had seen large breakers barging their way through the shallows. This one-mile passage, the Fornelli Pass, is just navigable in calm conditions carrying a maximum depth of barely three meters. It is often used by those making passage as it gives direct access from the Gulf of Asinara to the open Mediterranean. However, in current conditions, we would need to stay in deeper water and sail the longer 15-mile route round the rugged northern headland. I knew it would be rough and wet but hoped that the others would not be too worried.

Decision taken, we needed to get moving. Standing on the deck, I fought to secure all three reefs in the mainsail without raising it. Even within the relative protection of the small breakwater jutting into the bay the boat was yawing badly around the anchor chain. Shaunagh, Harry and Rosie cleared away all loose items below decks and secured the hatches. Ten minutes later, Harry and I did a final check before starting the engine and raising the anchor. When the anchor broke out of its grip on the weed and mud we immediately crabbed sideways towards the rough concrete blocks of the breakwater. I rapidly hoisted the reefed mainsail and unfurled a scrap of headsail as Shaunagh secured the anchor. We heeled over hard and, gathering speed, powered out from behind the secluded safety of the small harbour in Stintino.

The next hour was deceptive as, under triple reefed main and genoa, we pounded our way across the white-flecked waters in the lee of the island. However, I knew that once we rounded the headland looming ahead of us the sea state would become much worse. The vertical cliffs of the Asinara peninsular spat down vicious squalls which came swirling towards us as they ripped at the surface of the water and I wondered what was going through the others' minds. We were all silent, lost in our own thoughts, apprehensive of the open sea between this isolated corner of northern Sardinia and the Spanish coastline 240 miles away. Stuffing my Vendee Globe baseball hat firmly onto my head to avoid losing it overboard, I concentrated on helming the boat.

An hour later we rounded the headland. Conditions immediately deteriorated, making it almost impossible to see the crucial small buoy marking the reef that extended from the old lighthouse long since battered into ruins by generations of waves bursting against it. With increasing urgency and using two sets of binoculars we finally spotted the buoy. Once clearly past it, we slowly worked our way out into the open sea. Inexorably our speed over the ground dropped as we caught the full effect of the northwestly gale and the waves that were now beginning to break across the front of the boat. I steered off a few degrees to try and get a better wind angle on the sails but realised with silent concern that on such a heading we were now running parallel to a dangerous lee shore only three miles to port. Cursing myself, I realised the wind was too strong to point higher under sail alone. Turning the engine on, I started to pinch back into the wind to gain ground. Gradually, very gradually, we clawed our way to seaward. I kept the engine on until safely away from any potential hazard but even motor-sailing our heading was considerably south of what I wanted. The wind was too strong to sail higher. For a brief while I seriously considered turning back. By the time Shaunagh voiced the same question aloud we were four hours out and, by then, had gone too far to turn back. We were making ground, slowly and brutally.

For the next 38 hours, having cleared the Sardinian coastline, we stubbornly close-reached towards Menorca, substantially south of the heading I needed but the best I could achieve in such conditions. The wind never dropped below 30 knots. The forecast had been wrong. The short pitched waves, pushed up by the north-westerly gale over the last two days across 250 miles of open water, curled at us with foaming crests breaking over the boat and occasionally over the spray-hood soaking us all in slate-grey cold and salty water.

In such conditions, I have always found that most boats tell you about themselves, so long as you listen – not through your ears but through your hands and feet. Bernard Moitessier encapsulated sailing so well when he wrote, 'There is not much to do on a boat. But there is much to feel'. When that starts to happen it becomes a question of achieving the right balance between natural power and human input. Fathom and I seemed to find our balance early that afternoon. Thereafter, I sat high on the windward cockpit coaming watching and timing the onrush of each wave. At the bottom of every trough *Fathom* would slow and gather herself momentarily before pushing up the side of the oncoming wave. With a sudden lift and flip of her transom we slipped over the crest, the wave rolled under the hull and we surged down the front in a welter of foam and rushing water before slowing, pausing and starting the process all over again. Wave after wave was treated in the same fashion in rhythmic cadence. Only the occasional wave caught us badly and we would fall off the top of the wave with an almighty crash that once threw Shaunagh clean out of her berth and across the saloon. That first night, as darkness fell, the others went below to try and get some sleep. I stayed on the helm and spent most of the night gradually relaxing and learning the feel and rhythm of *Fathom* through my hands and feet.

It took a total of 71 hours before we tied up on the fuel jetty in our home marina. We had sailed more than 300 miles, over half of it in gale-force winds. I had snatched a total of seven hours' sleep. Whilst tired, I was pleased *Fathom* and I had sailed in such conditions as, after 42 years, the open ocean's siren call had finally become irresistible. In four months' time I was setting out from the Canary Islands to follow my father's transatlantic footsteps, all 2,900 miles of them, to Barbados. Genetics are interesting.

However, in my case I was going solo.

CHAPTER 1

THE PLANNING

*'We all have a need, mostly unsatisfied and rarely spoken,
to measure ourselves against nature as we were meant
to. To see how far our muscles and our breath and our
unaided minds can take us. In a culture that lets us do
little for ourselves we have this curious and hidden need
to make our way on our own two feet.'*
Reese Palley, There Be No Dragons

Why do it? – I asked myself that question many times
in the year before the trip. I was asked the same question by most of our friends and found I was unsure how
to reply. It's not everyday that a 50-year old who has
spent the last 30 years behind a desk in the City or
sardined on long distance flights decides to sail solo across
one of the world's great oceans. After a while I found
the best response was to shrug, smile lightly and say it
was the male menopause. It may sound a bit limp, but
it normally produced knowing looks and discouraged
further questioning.

The truth is that I had always had a nagging ambition for a transat which I dated back to my Oxford University days in the mid 1970s. Then, just after my first (losing) Boat Race in 1975 I had considered a transatlantic row. The physical challenge appealed along with the adrenalin buzz but, like many of my ideas then, it sank before the onslaught of a second Boat Race in 1977 with the largest winning margin in 75 years. Every member of the crew that year had represented their respective countries at international level but training 6 hours a day, 13 days a fortnight and 8 months of the year was still one of the most physically and mentally energising experiences for each of us. The downside was the level of physical training and commitment demanded for such an endurance race caused mayhem with crew relationships. As a result, whilst we completed the task successfully and professionally, we parted after the race rarely to see one another again. After that experience, in all things physically challenging I feel more comfortable relying on my own skill, strength and company. It is less complicated.

A second thread had been my father's own transatlantic in 1963 with Jinty Calvert, the girl who was later to become my stepmother. In *Heliousa,* a 39ft teak and iroko ketch built by the same builder as *Pamara,* they had crossed the Atlantic in December 1963. Motor sailing for 95% of the way he, Jinty and another crewman taken on for the crossing took 23 days to reach Barbados. They had set off from Las Palmas and it was my intention to follow roughly the same route, the classic downwind crossing using the prevailing north-easterly trade winds, aiming at their 23 days as an informal target to beat. The following year they crossed the Pacific to Brisbane. For part of that passage my father sailed the boat solo for 11 days and later told me that he had hated every moment. I was interested to see how deep the genes really went.

Whilst in 1963 my father had been 39, I was now 50 and my male menopause excuse had, probably, more than a grain of truth in it. For a while I had found I had been increasingly marking articles by those who had decided to go out and actually do something about fulfilling some personal ambitions long harboured but never actioned. That old adage of 'the only things in life you ever regret are those you should have done and never did' struck an enormous chord for me. The most poignant quote that I read shortly after my father died in November 2003 is in Joe Simpson's superb book, *The Beckoning Silence*:

'*Nobody grows old living a number of years, people grow old only by deserting their ideals. Years wrinkle the skin, but to give up enthusiasm wrinkles the soul. Worry, doubt, distrust, fear and despair . . . these are the long, long years that bow the head and turn the growing spirit back to dust. Whether seventy or sixteen, there is in every being's heart the love of wonder, the sweet amazement of the stars and star-like things and thoughts, the undaunted challenge of events, the unfailing child-like appetite for what is next, and the joy and game of life.*'

This passage encompassed so many emotions and seemed to evoke so many regrets about the swiftness of passing time. I knew that if I left it any longer such an ambition would just run the risk of sinking once more under the weight of expense, lack of time and general lethargy. This lack of enterprise was summed up by Libby Purves, who wrote about our western over-regulated handrail culture where *'a minority assert their rights to push their limits and risk their lives. The rest of us sink ever deeper into a fearful, torpid, timid, risk-averse culture which causes incalculable harm to health, education, mental balance, the spirit of enterprise, even the economy.'* Whilst somewhat overstated, I nevertheless felt that I was slowly becoming a member of the 'rest of us' group, all for very good family and financial reasons, but that in so doing I was subjugating the part of me that yearned to do something more physically and mentally challenging than spend my time managing part of a large business. My bathroom mirror had also been increasingly telling me that there really was a minimum acceptable level of physical self-esteem and which it and I both felt, upon reflection, had been reached and breached a few years earlier.

That said, I had no idea how I would react to three weeks alone in the wide oceanic waters of the Atlantic. I didn't quite subscribe to Nietzsche's *'what doesn't kill you makes you stronger'* but I was genuinely interested by the opportunity it would give me to observe my reactions.

I also felt strongly that doing something unusual like

this should be used as a way to raise money for others less fortunate than I have been in my life. A successful career and the privileges that it can bring are still too easily taken for granted. The City is also not an environment that has recently been readily associated with charitable giving, unfairly in some very notable cases, so it seemed to me appropriate to pass the hat around. The response and individual generosity was far more than I had ever expected. Additionally I reckoned that, if I ended up hating the whole thing by day three, I could hardly turn back and reimburse all my family, friends and colleagues who had so generously filled the hat from their own pockets. I would have to carry on. Accordingly, I asked Save the Children and a small special-needs school in Southwark, Beormund School, if they would be my chosen charities. Doing something for children emotionally challenged and less privileged than many at the outset of their lives seemed appropriate after my own working lifetime in the City. Working with representatives from Save The Children and the staff and children from Beormund was hugely rewarding, especially the latter who twice asked me down to their assembly to give presentations to the pupils and staff on the trip. After the first one, I was immensely touched to receive a book of wonderfully imaginative drawings from many of the pupils to encourage me on my way.

My family thought I was nuts. My beloved wife, Shaunagh, and all five of our children have always been quite open and direct in their opinions and it had taken some long talks with Shaunagh, and some memorably shorter ones, to win her agreement. I realised I was asking her to sacrifice a lot emotionally. Throughout all the subsequent planning she was wonderful both in terms of her visible and open support and for keeping her concerns largely unspoken. The only times the latter appeared was when well-meaning friends said, 'You're so brave' (to me) and, 'Aren't you worried?' (to her). Neither was helpful, neither added anything and both were unnecessary reminders of only the negative aspects of such a trip. How much nicer it would have been to hear, 'You're so lucky' (to me) or, 'Aren't you pissed off not to be going?' (to her). The response to both would have been, of course, yes.

We had originally considered doing the transat together but I found myself increasingly turning to the concept of a solo. Why? I longed to see if I could prove to myself before it was too late that I still had most of the physical and mental strength I enjoyed when rowing; I wanted to feel again the excitement of uncertainty; I wanted to experience and sail across one of the great oceans; above all, I wanted the buzz of achieving some-thing that I felt would really test my character and ability. I knew that to complete a transat in the company of others would not satisfy those feelings for me. The longer I thought about it the more I realised that I had to go alone. However, going alone made it more important that we were both fully committed to the trip as we realised the one left behind was likely to worry far more. Shaunagh also worried that my desire to go alone signi-fied some form of running away from her. As this was precisely what my father had done in 1963, I suppose it was a logical assumption. However, she was wrong. Having been together for 12 years we are very close and I would have found it impossible to contemplate such a trip without her support.

As a result, we agreed that I would take with me an Iridium satellite phone and speak briefly twice daily. These calls were largely to talk about what had happened during the day, how we were both getting on and the more mundane aspects of everyday family life. It helped both of us retain a sense of normality which, on a couple of occasions when things went wrong for me on the trip, I found immensely reassuring. From reading my father's memoirs of his Atlantic crossing I knew this had been an important psychological issue for him when he wrote:

'Jinty accused me of becoming addicted to fiddling with the wireless . . . it gave one something to do, but much more than this it gave one the illusion that one was still in touch with the world. Otherwise one felt like a traveller through space in a rocket without windows'

Taking the satellite phone was a great boost as another in a long list of worries I had before the trip was how I would react to the absence of hearing other voices. A box full of talking books including *My Way* (Bill Clinton), *My Trade* (Andrew Marr), *Himalaya* (Michael Palin), *The life of Pi* (Yann Martell), *A Short History of Almost Everything* (Bill Bryson), and *A Hitchhikers Guide to the Galaxy* (Douglas Adams) sat on the shelves alongside various CDs from John Cleese, Billy Connolly, Victor Borge and Peter Ustinov. As travelling companions go it was a great crew and I was constantly kept amused by their stories and humour. However, it was still not quite the same. Those twice daily calls to Shaunagh made all the difference even though the evening ones sometimes left me feeling emotionally flat.

Fathom herself was a 41ft French built GRP sloop, a Beneteau Oceanis 411, displacing 7.5 tons and in which I had sailed just under 3,000 miles since buying her 2 years earlier. I had spent three years looking for what I considered to be the right balance between affordability and sailing performance and was delighted to find that Beneteau produced such a well designed and responsive fast cruiser. The decision was made for me when we chartered a 411 in February 2002 in the Solent and had good testing Force 7 winds all weekend. With Shaunagh and two close friends we had a wonderful two days pounding across the near empty Solent before quietly sailing up the Beaulieu River to Buckler's Hard on a bright but chilly early February evening. As we moored alongside the pontoon, we spotted a deer emerge from the woods on the far side of the river. Silently it walked down to the water's edge, paused before slipping into the cold grey water and swam across almost under our bows to a small spit just ahead of us. Walking stiffly out of the water it shook itself so hard all four legs wobbled violently before trotting off into the nearest thicket. Sailing has its moments and this seemed a good omen.

I took delivery of *Fathom* almost exactly a year later in the spring of 2003. As we had bought a house in Catalunya three years earlier I had decided to berth her locally in Spain as the Mediterranean sailing season is so much longer than in the UK. She had been put on a low-loader from the factory in France near La Rochelle, brought over the Pyrenees and down the coastal motorway to Port Ginesta 15 kilometres south of Barcelona. I remember well sitting in my office in London when the broker called on that Thursday afternoon to say she had arrived but that no work would start on her until the following Monday morning. As I was flying out to Barcelona the next evening for the weekend (our house is some 70 miles north of the city), I decided I would detour on arrival at 11.30pm to go and find her so we could make formal introductions to one another and say quiet hellos.

I felt the thrill and excitement of a young boy as I drove south from the airport just before midnight. I was about to meet the boat that was going to sail with me across the Atlantic within the next two to three years. It was quite a thought. After getting briefly lost in the dark an all my excitement, I arrived at the marina gates but was stopped from entering in my car by a very sleepy guard at the barrier as I had no membership card. I parked by his cabin and walked the 300 meters to the darkened boats that stood around on their cradles between the sheds half covered in tarpaulins like small groups of adolescent hoodies lounging in unlit doorways on a Saturday night. It took me 10 minutes to find *Fathom* sitting on a trailer up against the side of a shed. I instantly recognised her outline from 50 meters away. With a huge grin on my face, I slowly walked two or three times

around her running my hand along the smooth surface
of her hull. Even standing on tip-toe, her deck was too
high for me to see properly and had been wrapped in
large sheet of pre-shrunk plastic for delivery. I sat down
by her keel and un-stepped mast. It was a great moment.
Far from seeming like some inanimate object stripped of
most of her fittings that remained packed away in featureless cardboard boxes stacked around her keel I instantly
felt a weird sense of character and occasion – not quite
a first date but a mutual flutter of recognition and more
than just a casual glance. It was as if I was meeting
someone for the first time but who I knew would become
a close friend. Having most of her 'bits' boxed and scat-
tered around like a part-built puzzle only made me all
the keener to see how she would finally look and feel.

Later, once complete and sea trialled, we started the
process of getting to know one another properly. Part of
this process is personal and often gives non-sailors ample
opportunity to make fun of the whole 'boating thing'.
Non-sailing friends of mine always seem to laugh about
boat names and gender. I never quite understand this as
I know a number of them who have cut their dogs balls
off and then given them ludicrous names which they
believe are side-splittingly funny. Of the two groups, it
seems obvious which is the better balanced. However, I
had read in one of Ellen MacArthur's books that to
personalise and give character to her boats she gave names
to various parts as it made her feel that she was not
completely alone on each of her extraordinary solo
achievements. I adopted the same principle. 'Otto' was

an obvious one for the Raymarine autopilot (ST6000) and without whose faultless performance I would have had a more exhausting time and 'VP' was the Volvo Penta main engine. However, 'Beast' was the cruising chute as it always provoked a relatively high degree of mental and physical effort to raise and lower each day whilst 'AA' (as in Alcoholics Anonymous) was a mid-Atlantic late entrant for the generator once I learned it drank a lot of fuel and would not function properly over 20 degrees of heel. What was the point? However, along with *Fathom* they were my immediate family, crew and assistants.

During this period of getting to know one another we experienced pretty much every type of weather. Whilst I was well aware that the Atlantic would be a bigger challenge than the Mediterranean and would produce surprises, *Fathom* had coped so well with all conditions to date that I felt confident we could successfully make the trip. Before buying her I had spent some time speaking with a couple of other 411 owners about their experiences and decided to put a third reef in the main, which proved extremely sound advice in winds above Force 6. For the transat I decided to add a removable inner forestay to carry a storm jib (used extensively by the crew who sailed *Fathom* back from the Caribbean after I had finished the transat). Two large emergency satellite beacons (EPIRBS) were fitted along with the 6kw diesel generator and a 6 man offshore emergency liferaft. In the two months leading up to the trip, she was anti-fouled, the 55hp Volvo engine fully serviced and new lifelines fitted. A rigger was arranged to give the rig a complete check-over. My only concern was whether to fit a wind vane as a back-up autopilot to Otto. However, the cost was quite high for a one-off and fitting a wind vane to the stern of *Fathom* with a sugar-scoop stern would have required a cat's cradle of attachments and supports. I decided to run the risk of relying solely on Otto and hope I had no electrical problems. The only other fitting I took a positive decision not to fit was a spinnaker pole with which to pole out the headsail. Whilst this is the chosen rig for most downwind sailing, I was not interested in having to move around on the foredeck manhandling a large pole and sheets on my own. In the event of a problem it was also not a rig that I could dismantle quickly without going forward. The risk did not seem worth taking as I was not racing and did not need the extra weight or worry.

At L'Estartit marina where I kept the boat, the local Nauticmar representative was responsible for ordering and overseeing all the work I needed for the trip, as my time was limited and he had looked after the boat for the last two seasons. After a long drawn-out series of increasingly bad-tempered meetings and emails and only two weeks before *Fathom* was due to sail for the Canaries with a delivery crew of close friends, he finally confirmed that all had been completed. As it turned out, this wasn't the case. Nauticmar is a big firm in Spain and must have been unaware just what a disservice their local branch did to their company. Sadly, the entire local boating fraternity told me only after my trip what a fool the representative was considered by all. It even transpired that he had failed to service the emergency liferaft although he had removed it from the boat to do so. He just took it away for two weeks and then returned it unopened and unserviced. This frightening truth only emerged when it was serviced 'again' in 2008 and the certificate in the container was examined. I was not surprised to find some months later that Nauticmar had closed their L'Estartit branch and delighted to see there was no sign of their erstwhile representative.

At the time I was unaware and anyway had no ready alternative. As it was, he sent my friends and I to sea, knowing what we were planning, without completing several of the checks but having charged me in full for them. Perhaps I was the greater fool. Happily the delivery crew of Malcolm Eyles, Paul Kibble and Glyn Davies were sufficiently experienced and had the time to double-check most things again during the run down to Las Palmas.

Whilst *Fathom* was supposedly having her final checks in Spain, I was busy rounding up my final cheques from friends for the charities. The generosity being shown by everybody towards the trip seemed to have caught on and was being led by my employers, Cazenove. They had given me two extra weeks off for the trip to add to the two weeks I was taking out of my holiday allowance. I had reckoned I would need a total of four weeks to allow sufficient time (plus a margin for an emergency or other problem) to get across and have a short recovery period in Barbados. Andrew Ross (CEO) had ensured a new heavy duty offshore cruising chute with Cazenove emblazoned all over it and Tim Steel (Chairman) had led the charge with a very generous personal contribution. With two large dealing floors full of psychotic dealers, Cazenove had even managed to promote an internal competition to guess the days and hours I would take with the closest guesstimate winning half the pot with the balance going to the charities. Additionally, a further 134 individuals had contributed towards a total that stood at a remarkable £40,000 by the time I started. Originally I had no idea as to how much might be raised and had rather hopefully aimed for £10 a mile for the 2,900 mile crossing. However, that was comfortably and generously exceeded. The total included a number of unexpected cheques, one of which was from Sir Richard Branson. Although I had never met him, I wrote a personal letter to him bearing in mind his own extensive record of adventuring. In the letter I asked whether Virgin Atlantic, with whom I had just booked two first-class tickets Barbados-London for my return with Shaunagh after the trip, would consider refunding 50% of the ticket price to the charities. He had responded personally, by return, confirming the refund. I was grateful and impressed.

Encouraged by the level of enthusiastic support, I started to explore the possibilities of setting up a transat website. The idea was to give family and friends a site that would not only track my daily progress on a chart but also to where I could also send emails directly from the boat. I ended up speaking with a small firm in New York

(Human Edge Technology) specialising in expedition software, originally developed for the Special Services. Using just a PDA and an Iridium satellite phone I could transmit any message, photograph and position directly from the boat to the website. It was something that gave me endless pleasure both during and after the trip and seemed to do likewise to a rather larger group of friends and colleagues than I had expected. Tom Sjogren, the founder of the company, was enormously helpful in teaching me from New York how the system worked. As a result I originally thought he was more a techie than an explorer – how wrong could I be. He and his wife turned out to have reached the North and South Poles as well as climbed Everest. Some couple. In London, I was given much time and support by Buster Drummond, a close friend of my stepson Harry. We spent several happy evenings with me sitting on my bed enthusiastically sending test messages via a satellite hundreds of miles above us to Buster three metres away in my bathroom.

By early October I was happy that most of my 'outstanding issues' list for the boat had been addressed. I then began a round of personal appointments with my optician, hygienist, dentist and doctor. Hardly any part of me remained free from prodding, poking and close examination. I was delighted to learn after all my hard work that my fitness was that of a fit 35 year-old whilst I was, perhaps, a bit less pleased to be told by my hygienist that my teeth were a disgrace. Given any choice between the two, however, I considered this the better way round.

I was as ready as I would ever be.

CHAPTER 2

LAS PALMAS

So, on Friday 25th November 2005, Shaunagh and I found ourselves landing in Las Palmas late in the evening 30 years after first conception, 3 years after buying the right boat, 2 years after the real planning started, 1 year after the physical training started and 6 months after reading *Your First Atlantic Crossing*. We had flown via Barcelona where we had just long enough on the ground to grab a quick lunch at Carmelitas in Calle Carmen behind the Boqueria. I was surprised at how calm I had been between leaving my office in the City the evening before (albeit I left quickly and quietly as rather too many colleagues had been coming to say goodbye and good luck) to getting up that morning and flying to Barcelona. We had a lovely lunch talking about nothing of any consequence but enjoying so much being on our own and in a city we both love.

It was only after we had taken the connecting flight and landed in Las Palmas and were driving in an unfamiliar taxi to an unknown hotel that I began to realise what I was about to do. In the dark, driving from the airport, I felt myself lurch emotionally and become, for a while, quite detached from my surroundings. I'm not one for great introspection preferring to get on with things rather than dwell on them. However, I realised that although we were both hiding it well, Shaunagh was feeling the strain too. An additional concern was that I had no idea if the boat had arrived and in one piece. The last message I had got from *Fathom* via satellite phone earlier in the week was that Malcolm, Glyn and Paul had experienced bad weather almost the entire delivery trip. This later turned out to be something of an understatement. At one stage they had been forced to heave-to for 12 hours in gale force winds some 300 miles south west of Gibraltar. That night, Glyn (an experienced sailor) had spent most of the night on his berth clutching the bolt-croppers convinced they would be hit by lightening and the mast would collapse – this towards the end of a trip in which they had only had two days of decent weather out of the 12 days it took to sail the boat 1,300 miles from her home port at L'Estartit marina in northeast Spain. However, the message had said they still expected to arrive nearly on schedule.

At the hotel, the 4-star Melia Las Palmas, Shaunagh and I checked in and dropped our bags in our room. Neither of us felt hungry but we both realised that an early night would probably only mean a sleepless one. Rather than be adventurous we decided to eat in the hotel and picked over a dinner in the rather too brightly lit and very unatmospheric restaurant. However, we did manage to sink a sufficient quantity to wine to make us relax enough to go to bed. Surprisingly, I think we both slept quite well until dawn.

When we got up, I checked my mobile messages and was relieved to see one from Malcolm:

Fathom in Las Palmas. All's well. Rgds Malc.

They had got in safely the previous night and were waiting for us down at the marina. I still have that one short message on my mobile today.

I was very keen to finish breakfast and get down to the marina. Shaunagh felt likewise but not before suggesting I fill my pockets with as many fresh bread rolls from the buffet as they could take. For some reason I found this a difficult suggestion as I had a peculiar sensation that this was not quite right even though we were paying a King's ransom for our two night stay. Trying hard not to look like some furtive schoolboy on a shoplifting trip I sauntered two or three times past the sideboard groaning under croissants, pain au chocolat, Danish pastries, loaves of every hue and seed and endless rolls. At each 'pass' I swept two rolls into my multi-pocketed jacket before turning round and repeating the process. Having stuffed 8 buns into various pockets, I headed off towards the exit convinced I was about to feel the grim grip of hotel security on my shoulder. I would never make a convincing thief, especially given the amount of flour that, unbeknownst to me, now covered my bulging jacket. As I walked past the waitress at the door I gave her what I thought was a winning and nonchalant smile. She must have thought me mad.

We walked down to the marina on a hot and sticky morning. As we got there I noticed all the ARC (Atlantic Rally for Cruisers) flags and pennants hanging limply on their poles around the quayside. They had been hung as part of the farewell ceremonies the previous Sunday as all 230 or so boats in the 2005 ARC Rally of all shapes and sizes had left Las Palmas for the annual transatlantic crossing en-masse to Antigua. I say en-masse but, in reality, all contact other than radio is lost amongst the participants within almost the first 48 hours as the fleet disperses across the vastness of the ocean. Because of the distance, the number of entrants and the range of experience it is the best known, and very probably, the best run of all such rallies. A high premium is placed by the organisers on safety and no boat is allowed to leave without a thorough inspection by one of their officers and a series of full briefings for all skippers. For many this would be the culmination of several years planning and, after crossing, they would either ship their boat back or sail the Atlantic circuit via the Caribbean, east coast of the USA and then back across the Atlantic via Bermuda and the Azores to make landfall somewhere on the European Atlantic seaboard. For a few it would be the start of a circumnavigation. All ARC entrants pay an entry fee but there are always a few other boats who try and tag on without paying the fee as they see the rally as providing free safety cover for their own crossing. They are jokingly referred to as NARCs (NOT Atlantic Rally for Cruisers) but are understandably considered irritants to organisers and paying entrants alike. I wanted to avoid such a label and, being solo, was not eligible to join the rally anyway. Accordingly, in all my plans I had specifically decided to leave a week later to give them time to get ahead of me to avoid worrying at night about running into rally back-markers.

The boys had made an early start. By the time Shaunagh and I found *Fathom* in the vast marina on pontoon Q they had tidied her so well you could hardly tell they had only got in the night before. A job list was being slowly and methodically completed, including a full rigging check. In the preceding months the Nauticmar agent in L'Estartit had twice confirmed he had checked and tightened the rigging. I had paid both invoices without having had the chance to sail *Fathom* after the last confirmed check, just two days before departure. However, it became instantly obvious to the boys on their departure from L'Estartit that this last check had never been done. Throughout their 12 day run to Las Palmas they said they nursed the boat more than sailed it. When the Beneteau agent in Las Palmas came to inspect it he confirmed the rigging had not been touched recently. We did it ourselves. The various jobs completed, the boat checked over and my kit stowed, we all went out for a quick lunch. With my mind occupied by immediate needs, the nerves and emotional lurching of the previous evening evaporated.

After lunch, Shaunagh wanted to complete the 'final' round of food shopping. After visiting an open-air vegetable market we opted instead for the convenience of the nearby air-conditioned Corte Ingles food hall. Now, for anyone who knows my wife, you will appreciate that advance culinary planning for the trip had started some months earlier. By the time the boat reached Las Palmas provisioning was impressive. Energy bars, vitamin supplements, powdered carbohydrate drinks, various disgusting-tasting dietary supplements and pills of every description had been stowed in one of the larger lockers; in another had been piled lentils, rice of every hue and colour, pumpernickel, rye bread, cress seeds, split peas, black beans, kidney beans and every other type of bean available. When my brother-in-law and I had loaded the initial supplies in Spain, noting each item of food as it was stowed, he expressed some considerable concern over my wellbeing if (1) I managed to eat even half of what Shaunagh had provisioned and (2) I did not spend most of the journey doubled up with wind. Certainly if there was none I could make my own. Enough pasta to feed the Italian navy had been boxed into the aft berth whilst tins of tuna, sweet-corn, anchovies, vegetables and fruit were stowed under the main berth. The jars of mayonnaise, patés, Tabasco, Marmite, marmalade, plum jam, apricot jam and honey were split between the bilges and various small lockers in the saloon (which meant I could never find the one I wanted) and, finally, the beer, wine and spirits were hidden from public view to save me any personal embarrassment. The only possible space left available on board were the fridge and small freezer. Accordingly Shaunagh collected two vast trolleys of chicken, lamb, beef, butter, milk, Greek yoghurt, smoked salmon, ham, mackerel fillets and chocolate bars for the fridge/ freezer whilst the apples, bananas, oranges, tangerines, tomatoes, onions, garlic, lettuces, carrots and potatoes were put into bulging net bags strung the whole way around the galley. My only contribution, two fruit cakes, I managed to squash behind the stewing pot in which Shaunagh had bubble wrapped two dozen eggs. I didn't expect to starve.

Having completed all the final stowing, Shaunagh and I went back to the hotel for a bath before all meeting in the hotel lobby for a drink. I say 'a bath' as in reality it was one of those continental size baths that the British find so odd and in which body parts have to take turns to get wet. Being six foot six inches in height, it amused me to observe that I was likely to be more comfortable washing over the next three weeks on a boat than I was currently in a four star hotel ashore.

After drinks we followed a recommendation and found a fish restaurant overlooking the sea a short walk from the hotel. We had a very relaxed dinner, opting for the 'menu del dia' which seemed to be grilled fish of the boniest type available in that part of the Atlantic. Between alternating mouthfuls of bone and local wine conversation became steadily more animated as the evening wore on. Finally, we all wandered somewhat unsteadily back along the sea-front towards our hotel (the boys were sleeping on the boat) making our farewells and thank-yous to Glyn who was leaving very early the following morning. Everyone seemed relaxed. That night Shaunagh and I went to bed in one another's arms, for what we both privately wondered could perhaps be the last time, without either being badly worried.

I woke before dawn with a checklist of practical issues already running through my mind. Around 8am we got up quietly and went down for breakfast. We were both subdued. After yesterday's furtive behaviour by the bread counter I concentrated on trying to eat as much as possible. I realised this would be my last chance to relax over bacon, eggs and black coffee until I reached Barbados. I also realised it would be the last time Shaunagh and I had a few quiet moments together and to enjoy them. Back in London, when leaving the house for the flights to Las Palmas two days earlier, I had quietly propped a letter on her pillow. In it I had tried to explain how much she meant to me and how much I appreciated her understanding and support throughout the whole project. I had found it a difficult letter to write as I am not good at expressing my emotions and did not want to frighten her by leaving a 'last' letter. Somehow I had managed to script something that did not seem to fall over the cliff of sentimentality nor sound too much like a suicide note. It gave me some emotional comfort to know she would find it when she returned to London late that evening.

After a quick last look at a couple of internet websites for the latest weather forecast in the Hotel's business centre we checked out and took a taxi to the marina.

CHAPTER 3
THE TRANSAT

I think everyone was keen to get the goodbyes over and we all seemed somewhat brusque. It only took 15 minutes to get ready. Bags were handed ashore, fixed smiles were maintained, last-minute words were exchanged in subdued voices and with minimum fuss and after a couple of photographs and only the briefest of hugs with Shaunagh I started the engine and cast off all lines. Slowly I edged *Fathom* out of her berth between an aging catamaran and a deserted sloop. In glassy conditions I motored towards the two small beacons that marked the exit from the marina. As I passed them, I knew with utter certainty, that I was moving from the security and safety of a man-made environment into the unknown. My emotions were sharply focused and very mixed – glad and relieved to be under way but completely unable to look back.

I timed my departure from the berth on the Muelle

Deportiva, Las Palmas at 09.52 on the 27th November 2005.

Once clear of the marina breakwater and under a cloudless blue sky with only the lightest of winds from the northeast, I flicked Otto on and went forward to remove and stow all the fenders and put up both full main and genoa. Standing there on the deck quietly coiling the ropes and preparing the boat I pushed any remaining butterflies aside and felt a sudden sense of relief and purpose. The planning had taken 18 months of increasing pressure and time. To find myself now actually wandering about *Fathom* confidently putting things away that I knew I would not see or use until eventual arrival in Barbados made me feel quite a salty sea-dog. Daft I know, and (personally) a feeling I felt quite unfounded, but it was a small thrill. I think I also busied myself purposefully as I was finding it very hard to think of the small group of Shaunagh, Malcolm and Paul on the pontoon 500 metres behind me collecting their bags and cases and walking slowly back towards the waiting taxi. Shaunagh had surprised me in her control as I knew she was finding this bit far harder than I was. My gratitude, though silent, was very real as it had allowed me to concentrate on getting myself sorted without added distraction. Thankful, although unable to show it, I fully realised how much more difficult it was for her to be the one left behind. I was also deeply grateful she was flying back with Paul and Malcolm for company. In an effort to lighten her mood I remember sending her a text message from the boat as she was driving to the airport saying:

Haven't hit anything yet. Does anyone know what Barbados looks like?

I'm not sure it worked.

I made slow progress down the east side of Gran Canaria. Shaunagh called me once briefly as she, Malcolm and Paul were boarding their return flight. She also sent me a text to my mobile:

We watched you sail out all the way to the airport. Dead jealous of sun, sea & love you.

Which, again, I saved in my inbox and still have today. 20 minutes later, when abreast of the airport on the southern tip of the Island, I stood up and looked astern as I heard their aircraft thunder down the runway and climb lazily into a hazy sky before turning to the north-east. Holding on to the backstay, I stared at the rapidly disappearing dot in the sky. After less than a minute my straining eyes and ears could no longer see the tiny shape nor hear any engine noise. I stood there for a while in the silence before turning round and sitting down in the cockpit. It was a strange moment – after two years planning and a lifetime of dreaming I was now committed, finally, to my adventure. I was completely alone and was leaving behind everything and everyone I loved and heading into the vast openness of the Atlantic. There, I would be completely dependent upon *Fathom*, myself and with only what I had on board. I stared at the horizon and with a surge of adrenalin thought of the 2,900 miles that lay ahead.

To avoid emotional air-pockets I made myself get up and rig a solution to something that had worried me for a while. In the months of planning my one recurring fear had been falling or being washed overboard. I had given Shaunagh a solemn and firm undertaking that I would wear my safety harness clipped on to the jackstays whenever leaving the relative safety of the cockpit. The jackstays are strong webbing straps that run full length down either side of the boat along the deck and are bolted securely at either end. However, I was much more worried that, even if clipped on, falling or being washed over the side would only keep me attached to the boat and no more. There was the distinctly more interesting and infinitely more challenging practical problem of how then to get back on board. Assuming the safety line did not snap as I went over the side and that I broke no bones in the process, the deck was three feet above sea level and the stanchions and double guard rails were at least another couple of feet above that. There was absolutely no way I would be able to haul myself five feet vertically out of the water in wet clothing whilst being dragged along by the boat in bad weather. It was also quite unrealistic to believe I could slowly work my way aft whilst still attached to my safety line as, to do so, I would have to lift myself sufficiently far out of the water at each stanchion to lift my safety line over the top of each one. I had nasty mental images of the boat being found two months later with desiccated bits of me still attached to it half way along the waterline having been unable to get back on board. So, the first thing I did was attach two ropes down either side of the boat on the outside of all obstructions and secured to the bow, amid-ship and aft cleats. I left sufficient slack in both lines that they could be grabbed from sea level and pulled overboard to provide some form foothold to climb back onboard. *In extremis* I could unclip my safety line and hand my way aft using the rope until I could climb aboard from the stern. It surprises me that, for whatever reason, I have never seen this raised as an issue by other solo sailors.

Once finished on deck I went below to complete my final stowing. Whilst we had all taken every care to put items into lockers before departure it amazed me at how much loose clutter still existed. There were one or two carrier bags of last minute purchases lying on the saloon floor, my bright yellow waterproof Pelican cases containing laptop, cameras and Iridium phone were all jammed together in the main cabin making the forward heads inaccessible and a variety of papers and reference books lay all over the navigation station. To top it all, the white sheep's fleece Shaunagh had given me to use in the cockpit to avoid getting salt-water sores lay on top of a pile of cockpit cushions – somehow I had felt that they had looked out of place for a boat setting out to cross the Atlantic rather than the Solent – making the whole ensemble look like a badly made Christmas cake. Stuffing as many of the items I could into the last available free space (there wasn't any), I returned as quickly as I could to the cockpit for safety's sake and to try and relax my nerves in the new surroundings. A light south-easterly force 3 pushed me down the east side of the island at little more than 3 knots in a gentle swell.

I saw my first pod of dolphins as I drew level with the lighthouse on the southern tip of the island and, as the sea floor dropped away below 200 metres and my depth gauge stopped giving me a reading, I decided to put the engine on to clear the island and as much shipping before dusk. I was also alert to the possibility of sudden strong gusts which I knew are often experienced downwind of the Canary Islands, caused by the islands' wind shadows compressing and accelerating wind eddies with little forewarning. Sailing where we live in Spain in the Golf de Lion the local Tramuntana (what the French call the Mistral) does likewise as the north-westerly winds become compressed through the gap between the Alps and the Pyrenees. I had quite enough experience of the effect these could have and I wanted no nasty scares this early on. I turned the engine on for the next four hours until it got dark when I switched it off and rigged *Fathom* for our first night at sea.

The first night at sea on passage, whether alone or with family, always gives me a sense of adventure and of entering an alternative world. I love night sailing, what Moitessier called 'the religion of nights at sea', with the peacefulness that darkness often brings and the disappearance of immediate horizons offset by the celestial Cathedral roof of the night sky above. I am also never able to resist the immense buzz that adrenalin produces, conditioned I am sure from my rowing days and the controlled energy and focus it provided before each race. Tonight felt very similar and once I had gone below after sunset to make something to eat I realised that I had lost all form of hunger. The adrenalin had also made me feel restless. Half-heartedly I opened some pate and turned the gas hob on for a tin of beans. For some reason I remember videoing this first attempt at self-catering before forcing a little of both down along with a can of diet coke. Shortly afterwards I wondered if the nagging feeling of nausea was due to this formidable combination or just general levels of subdued excitement and anticipation.

I am very lucky and have never suffered from sea-sickness (to date), irrespective of conditions. Occasionally I have been offshore in big seas and stayed below long enough to realise I should get back on deck and breathe fresh air but have luckily escaped the awfulness of proper, full blown sea-sickness. My father once told me there were three stages of the affliction – when you thought you were going to die, when you hoped you were going to die and, finally, when you became desperately worried you weren't going to die. Anyone who has sailed and suffered could empathise with each stage and I have seen many a crewman draped over the back of a boat like a soiled duvet motionless in the abject misery of a heaving sea, a heaving boat and a heaving stomach.

How much of my escape from such attacks was due to being put into the bottom of boats from a very early age as a child alongside the picnic hamper, spare life jackets, salty warps, fenders and equally small sister or brother is hard to tell. Both my parents were keen and experienced sailors and most summer weekends (or so it seemed to me) were spent as ballast in the bilges of a bewildering assortment of large wooden boats belonging to various friends, relatives and fellow Guards Yacht Club members. Some had engines which normally promised a relaxed sail whilst others were engineless and were dreaded by us children. Outings in these latter monsters, supposedly more peaceful through lack of mechanical smells and noise, were the exact opposite with departure from and return to the mooring anything but peaceful. Sailing large and heavy wooden boats on and off moorings in tidal and often windy conditions always seemed to result in enormously energetic shouting by whoever was on the helm and/or armed with a boathook. Crouched in the bilges, the pounding of feet back and forth on the decking above our heads always suggested looming disaster to my sister, brother and me and we spent much of the time braced for a crash. Happily, that never happened. The only time I remember my father ever making a very public display of uncharacteristic incompetence was in Italy when he had to suddenly reverse *Pamara*, all 79ft of her, in a rather narrow and confined harbour to avoid crushing a small boat that had manoeuvred across his bows. Unfortunately, although he missed the boat in front he reversed right over our own dinghy that was bobbing behind us attached to *Pamara's* stern by a nylon painter. With a ghastly splintering the tender disappeared under the stern faster than a dropped anchor whilst the painter equally rapidly disappeared into the threshing blades of the propeller still hard astern. To the sounds of grinding gears and nylon rope stretching to breaking point the propeller wound to a shuddering halt and the engine stalled. A complete silence descended on the harbour.

Slowly, in the light afternoon breeze, *Pamara* drifted powerlessly but sedately across the harbour entrance. It took 30 minutes for very expensive negotiations to be concluded between my irate father, an officious harbour master and the opportunistic skipper of a local fishing boat before the entrance was cleared and *Pamara* was pulled off and moored safely to the adjacent concrete pier.

It was a classic lesson in why sailors need to anticipate the unexpected.

Sadly that was a lesson I appeared to have forgotten. Amongst all the activity and tension of the last 12 hours, much to my imminent physical discomfort, I had forgotten to check my email inbox. I had spent an hour that morning and the previous evening going through all my normal online weather sites and their forecasts had all been fine for the Canaries. However, I was aware that a tropical storm, officially designated Delta, was lurking mid-Atlantic, making slow progress north-eastwards. It had first shown up four days previously and the 200 boat ARC fleet had been advised to head south to avoid any unwanted effects. The fleet immediately split into two groups with the cruisers pushing slowly south whilst the racers drove due west to try and climb above the deep low pressure system and pick up the stronger winds. A number in the latter group were to regret that decision. Leaving a week after them, I thought a prompt departure would give me time to make as much southing as possible during the first 24 hours and to duck under any major disturbance caused by the storm. I was also quite keen to get distance from the 24 assorted rowers scheduled to leave Gomera, another island 15 miles to my west, in the 2005 Woodvale Transatlantic (rowing) Race to Antigua. Most of them intended to row naked to avoid sea sores, including Roz Savage, the lone intrepid female rower, and I'm not sure I could have dealt with such a surrealist scene this early in the trip. Reminds me of the Monty Python...... and now for something completely different'. However, my youngest daughter, Rosie, had insisted I keep a camera at the ready at all times in case I passed James Cracknell, the Olympic double gold medallist, and Ben Fogle in their pair.

That night, mindful of being within the shipping lanes, I tried to take short catnaps but the adrenalin that had killed my appetite also kept me wide awake. Instead, I sat quietly in the cockpit sensing the first long rhythmic breaths of the Atlantic swell under a star-filled sky and glimpsing occasional lights from distant fishing boats and freighters. I was surprised how quickly they disappeared after midnight. In the early hours, turning the radar on for short bursts, I saw that I was already on my own up to a radius of 16 miles and, after that, I did not see any more lights. However, what I had started to notice was that the night sky was becoming increasingly obscured by high cloud. At that stage, I didn't think much about it.

28 Nov – 11:57 GPS – pos: N26°14' | W016°17'

Distance covered in previous 24 hours	109 nm
Crispin Latymer (CL) total	109 nm
Hugo Latymer (HL) total	126 nm
+/–	17 nm

I cat-napped in the cockpit for some of the night but gave up trying to sleep properly just before dawn. I decided a cup of strong black coffee would be more useful. Overnight the wind had been moderate but as from 05.00hrs it started to swing from ESE to S and then to SW. As it swung, ominously it started to pick up strength. Throughout the morning I found myself watching high cirrus clouds coming in from the west and continuously reducing sail until, around midday, I had the minimum sail area of 3 reefs in both main and genoa. By then the wind was steady at over 30 knots and with a 9–12ft sea. I quickly took some more footage on my video where my voice was barely audible on the soundtrack over the noise of the wind. I was under-canvassed but knew I had a long way to go and didn't want to break anything this early on. I also wanted to try and work out quite what was happening as my onboard Navtex had been buzzing with increasing frequency and announcing strengthening winds.

Around midday I received the first gale warning.

TROPICAL STORM DELTA ADVISORY NUMBER 20 NWS TPC/NATIONAL HURRICANE CENTER MIAMI FL 11 AM AST MON NOV 28 2005

AT 11 AM AST . . . 1500Z . . . THE CENTER OF TROPICAL STORM DELTA WAS LOCATED NEAR LATITUDE 30.3 NORTH . . . LONGITUDE 20.1 WEST OR ABOUT 175 MILES . . . 285 KM . . . NORTHWEST OF LAS PALMA IN THE CANARY ISLANDS AND ABOUT 250 MILES . . . 400 KM SOUTHWEST OF FUNCHAL IN THE MADEIRA ISLANDS.

DELTA IS MOVING TOWARD THE EAST NEAR 30

MPH ... 48 KM/HR ... AND THIS MOTION IS EXPECTED TO CONTINUE FOR THE NEXT 24 HOURS. ON THE FORECAST TRACK ... DELTA IS EXPECTED TO PASS BETWEEN THE CANARY AND MADEIRA ISLANDS LATER TODAY AND EARLY TONIGHT ... AND REACH THE CENTRAL COAST OF MOROCCO BY TUESDAY MORNING.

MAXIMUM SUSTAINED WINDS ARE NEAR 65 MPH ... 100 KM/HR ... WITH HIGHER GUSTS. LITTLE CHANGE IN STRENGTH IS FORECAST DURING THE NEXT 24 HOURS. GALE- TO STORM-FORCE WINDS COULD OCCUR OVER PORTIONS OF THE CANARY AND MADEIRA ISLANDS LATER TODAY ... AND ALONG THE COAST OF MOROCCO AND NORTHERN MAURITANIA ON TUESDAY. WINDS WILL BE STRONGER OVER HIGHER TERRAIN.

TROPICAL STORM FORCE WINDS EXTEND OUTWARD UP TO 175 MILES ... 280 KM FROM THE CENTER.

THE ESTIMATED MINIMUM CENTRAL PRESSURE IS 988 MB ... 29.18 INCHES.

That was confirmation enough that conditions were deteriorating and was worryingly unwelcome. The same message also included a request to keep an emergency watch for a boat containing illegal African immigrants last seen in open seas heading for the Canary Islands. Mindful that these were not the conditions the medium-range forecast had predicted before I left, I hove to at 17.30hrs and put a satellite call through on the Iridium telephone to Simon Keeling at the Atlantic Weather Centre (AWC) in London. Over the phone he asked me to confirm my position and then, when told, expressed surprise that I had left Las Palmas. He had emailed me 18 hours earlier to recommend I delay my departure for at least 48 hours as the storm was deepening again, had changed direction and was now coming due east with increasing speed. I never read that email.

Both of us realised my situation. We also both knew there was nothing that I could do about it. Quickly but calmly we discussed the forecast and how the centre of the storm was now expected to pass only 150 miles to my north between Madeira and the Canary Islands. Simon asked me to confirm my current conditions and then, after a minute or so, told me to expect the winds to increase further overnight gusting over 50 knots. He also forecast the sea state to increase to 20–25ft with the possibility of 30ft by dawn. The one piece of good news was that as the storm was moving so quickly the wind shift from SW to NW should come through by 05.00hrs. That would at least bring the wind abeam. However, it would also create the possibility of dangerous cross-seas developing as the sea and wind, by then coming from different directions, would fight for dominance. It was, overall, an unnerving and sobering conversation and ended with Simon wishing me luck.

I sat for a few minutes at the navigation station lost in thought. I felt strangely detached from what was going on outside and concentrated instead on working out what I saw as the safest option. I felt there were only two –

heave-to or take down all sail and lie a'hull. I cursed myself for rigging the removable inner-forestay the day before and not leaving it lashed out of the way to one of the shrouds. Because of that, the genoa when backed, as it was now, was hard up against the inner-forestay. Given conditions and the forecast, it wouldn't take long to chafe right through the sail and leave it in tatters. I could have retrieved and hanked on the bright orange storm jib that, along with its sheets, was in the cockpit locker but amongst a mountain of spare kit and supplies. The speed with which conditions were now deteriorating and the increasingly abrupt movement of the boat made that a very borderline option. Realistically I felt I only had one practical choice. Calmly but quickly I decided I had to take down all sail and lie a'hull through the night and sit out the worst of the storm.

Looking back on that decision I would have no hesitation in making the same assessment again. I was less than 48 hours into a 2,900 mile trip, on my own and about to face the worst conditions I had ever experienced at sea. I was already tired after the mental pressures of the last few weeks and whilst confident that *Fathom* was capable of handling the conditions, I saw little point in taking a gamble for the sake of being blown backwards overnight and loosing sea miles. I had ample sea-room to leeward as the African coastline was 100 miles downwind and estimated that, at most, I should be blown downwind no more than 30 miles or so before dawn.

Clipping on my safety line, I climbed back into the cockpit to haul down all sail.

Even in the 15 minutes it had taken to put the call through and talk with Simon conditions had worsened. With light fast fading I clipped on, crawled out of the cockpit and scrambled forward on my hands and knees as the boat lurched and rolled. Soaked by the time I reached the mast, I climbed to my feet. It was only then that I remember noticing, with a mixture of awe and fascination, an ominous presence across the whole western horizon of a distended and swollen mass of dark cloud. It hadn't been there 15 minutes ago. I tried to estimate how much time I had before it arrived and realised it would not be long. Struggling to keep my balance on the very wet and, by now, heavily pitching coach roof I worked my way slowly down the boom, wrestling to lower what little of the main I still had up. Even with lazy-jacks and the main sheet hardened in it was not easy. The boom swung badly as *Fathom* rolled heavily in what was now becoming frequent breaking seas. My hands struggled to grab and hold the flogging sail whilst also trying to secure the sail-bag ties that I held in my mouth and which would hold down the whole mass of sail and canvas sail-bag. A couple of mis-timed scrambling slips across the coach-roof clutching boom, sail and loose reefing lines caught me off-balance but, finally, I had it all secured. Dropping to my knees and crawling back to the cockpit dragging my life-line with me I collected some short lengths of rope. Reluctantly, I went forward once more and tied extra lashings around boom and sail to make certain nothing could work loose. I wanted to avoid any unnecessary damage and anything requiring me to go forward again. Dropping back to my knees, surprisingly breathless, I slid back once more into the cockpit, set and locked the wheel amidships, cleared away all loose items and fell, more than sat, on one side of the cockpit to watch how *Fathom* would behave.

Sitting there a'hull, with no sails up in the midst of a rising storm, I tried to keep my mind on what else I could do. I had ample warps to trail astern if needed. I had never believed in streaming sea anchors from the bows on boats with spade rudders as *Fathom* had. They seemed to expose the dangers of having a large unprotected rudder. In the event of a sudden backward surge caused by taking a breaking wave on the bow all the pressure would be taken by the rudder post which is rarely designed for such extreme loads. I had read too many stories of broken rudder posts and the consequences. I sat there for about five minutes gauging *Fathom's* behaviour. I was relieved to see that she seemed to be taking each wave reasonably naturally, lying bows down from the wind, and was drifting downwind at just under two knots. It didn't seem that she needed any more help from me. With a last look around, I went below.

I was cold, wet, still somewhat breathless and apprehensive.

Locking the lower washboard in position I sat on the quarter-berth for a while getting my breath back. For a while I listened to the noise of the wind outside wondering what the night would bring. For those not used to the sound of strong wind at sea and the noise it makes in the rigging it can be quite disorienting, especially at night.

It howls like a distant pack of wild animals. I had lived with that noise since around 06.00hrs that morning but with an increasing intensity as the day wore on. Now, as I sat there, the howl had become continuous and drowned out almost every other sound. I could also feel the unseen wind starting to push at the rigging and the mast. As each gust caught us, *Fathom* heeled and a much higher-pitched wail would momentarily drown out the only other identifiable sound of halyards vibrating furiously against the aluminium mast. The sea was already rougher than an hour earlier and *Fathom* was starting to get caught off-balance by some of the larger and more aggressive waves as they broke against and over her. Conditions were becoming malevolent and, given the forecast, I knew they would only get worse.

Starting to remove my boots and wet weather kit I was suddenly seized by a sharp and piercing pain right across the side of my chest. It took my breath away. More cautiously, I slowly removed my outer wet weather clothes and then my shirt. Standing and moving to under one of the lights by the nav station I could see a dark blue-red mark across the right side of my rib cage. Prodding gently I realised I had just cracked or broken one or more ribs. With the coach roof awash with spray and *Fathom* rolling badly I must have been caught by the boom across the ribs while bagging the main. My concentration had been so focused that I hadn't even noticed at the time. Bugger! Less than one day out and already a problem. I had expected things to break sometime during the trip but I had thought it would be equipment, not bits of me and not so soon.

Knowing there was little I could do about damaged ribs, I carefully changed into dry clothes, took two paracetemol and wedged myself into the corner of a berth with some biscuits and a bottle of water. It was going to be a long night.

The first gust over 50 knots hit 20 minutes later.

29 Nov – GPS – pos: N25°40' | W017°05'

Distance covered in previous 24 hours	63 nm
CL total	172 nm
HL total	252 nm
+/-	–80 nm

Throughout the night the sea built to 25ft, pushed hard by storm force south-westerly winds. Wedged in my corner I dozed fitfully with sore ribs waking me as each gust literally hit *Fathom* in a blast of spray and foam. Perhaps strangely, at no stage did I feel alarmed. It was the worst conditions I had experienced and from below decks I knew I was considerably cocooned from what was happening outside. We were being rolled around quite badly but, not having put out a drogue or trailed warps, *Fathom* seemed to be maintaining her position of lying quite naturally bows down approximately 130 degrees off the wind. In this position the waves were coming at her stern quarter and she took them, for the most part, with an element of control.

The night was very dark, with heavy rain squalls continually sweeping the boat. The wind wailed ceaselessly through the rigging as if disappointed not to find any sails offering resistance. The incessant and violent sounds of the rigging and halyards being shaken against taut sheets and vibrating down the mast through the whole boat inhibited any sense of relaxation. I only went on deck once, at 02.30hrs, when I noticed my starboard lifebuoy and safety lamp were missing. Putting on my wet-weather jacket and safety harness I removed the lower washboard I had locked in place at the top of the companionway, slid back the hatch and clipped onto the nearest fixed safety bolt at the top of the companionway. Quickly but apprehensively I climbed into the dark. Heavy cold spray flew into and across the cockpit, instantly soaking me and making my thin trousers cling to me. With salt water running straight into my eyes I could see very little but in the darkness all around me was the sound of rampaging waves battling with gusting storm force winds. Looking quickly around the boat checking for signs of any problems I spotted, half-submerged behind the boat, a dim light blinking inter-mittently in the foam and spray. Realising with relief this was the lifebuoy and lamp tangled and trailing in the danbuoy lanyard I knelt down in the semi-shelter of the cockpit and hauled them both back on board. Once recov-ered, I saw it must have taken quite a wave to dislodge both as the wire fitting on the pushpit that had held them was a twisted mess. I tied them as best I could to the rail and retreated below decks shivering and soaked.

Movement below decks made it impossible to make any hot drink to warm myself so, after a rib-challenging change into dry clothes, I wedged myself back into the quarter berth and waited. Throughout the early hours I remember continually looking at my watch hoping for the wind shift. At 03.30hrs I noted in my log the temporary loss of the signals from both my radar and chartplotter whilst, at 04.30hrs, I became almost monosyllabic and just wrote *'Bad night'*. At 05.00hrs the wind shift started and the wind went north-westerly properly by 05.30hrs. I waited for dawn.

At first light the scene outside was awesome – an endless panorama of big breaking seas as far as the eye could see. The largest waves were topping out around 30 feet and moving as fast as articulated trucks on a motorway – literally millions of tonnes of water driven on by storm-force winds. Whilst all were breaking, few were breaking for more than a metre of their crests so did not seem to pose an immediate worry. However, I decided to wait a while longer for conditions to become less extreme before hoisting any sail.

A couple of hours later, at 08.30hrs my log entry was *'Big seas to 25 ft still'* but, although still noisy and rough, the sea was beginning to moderate and broken skies were appearing from the north-west as the wind decreased to force 7. Tired from my second night with little sleep but realising it was time to move on, I struggled painfully into full wet weather kit, went on deck and set triple reefs all round.

The memory of the next 12 hours will stay with me for the rest of my life. Wearing two safety lines independently clipped to two different cockpit safety rings, I manually hauled the reefed main aloft and unfurled a scrap of headsail. Released from her bruising night of inactivity, *Fathom* responded instantly. In a welter of spray and solid water her sails bit into the wind. Heeling under the power unleashed we accelerated and began beam-reaching across a liquid landscape of foaming green hills and deep valleys. Under a brightening blue sky the noisy and chaotic remnants of last night's elemental fight surged and collapsed all around us. As far as the eye could see, jagged white crests tumbled down the front of endless waves still raging across the ocean's surface. It was awe-inspiring to be in the middle of such wild scenery and I experienced a raw exhilaration and sense of freedom. Strangely, I do not remember feeling exposed or frightened even though, initially, I was more under water than on top of it. Instead, with a huge grin on my face and with seawater bursting over both *Fathom* and me we sailed between, over and down these great Atlantic waves at barely controllable speeds of up to 10 knots. It was breathtaking to be in the middle of the sheer power created by the storm and yet be able to harness some of it. *Fathom* was perfectly balanced as we twisted our way up the face of endless on-rushing waves and then raced off their backs as they rolled under us. I was filled with a huge childlike thrill of excitement and, after resisting the initial impulse, let out three great howls into the empty vastness of the ocean. In that one moment my mind seemed to let go of everything – every worry, every care, every responsibility – as if a slate was somehow being washed clean by the wild water all around us, and with it came an intense sense of freedom.

I had only one real moment of concern. I crested one particularly big wave and saw, in the next one racing towards us, a large opaque shape just under the surface. I have no idea what it was. I only had a quick sighting but it was about the same size as *Fathom*, dark grey in colour and looked somewhat irregular in shape. I was instantly alert to the possibility of semi-submerged metal containers. Given the appalling weather of the previous 12 hours and the fact I was still within the shipping lanes around the Canaries it was highly possible for a freighter to have lost containers over the side in the storm. It could also have been a whale or some other large marine animal. Whatever it was, I realised that at the speed I was going I would be ripped opened like a tin can and sunk within minutes if I hit such a solid obstacle. As there was little chance of slowing *Fathom* down all I could do was helm standing up in the hope my reactions would be fast enough if I saw another such obstacle ahead of me. Realistically, though, I knew that at the speed I was sailing and given the size of each wave any advance warning would have been minimal.

For a while I forgot my excitement and it became anxious, wet and tiring work in a cockpit that was constantly lurching and falling off waves. Then, as if to confirm my concerns, in the late afternoon a large freighter slowly punched its way through the seas some three miles ahead of me, rhythmically appearing and disappearing as *Fathom* crested each wave and then, spray covered, raced into each trough.

Finally, just before dusk, conditions had subsided

sufficiently for me to relax a bit. Although still lively, the sea had become more regular and the wind had dropped to a middling force 6. Having hand-helmed all day I was aching for a rest and to hand over to Otto.

More than anything else I needed a break as throughout the day I had been unable to get below and grab anything to eat. Additionally, any 'natural' urges had been resisted or had required the bucket. Under more normal circumstances this would have been quite funny as it required delicate timing and balance. Being a bloke is difficult at the best of times but with one hand on the helm and one on the bucket I ran out of hands with which to hold anything else. It took me a while to work out an alternative solution and sitting on a small bucket was not one of them – I tried, but crouched sideways in the cramped space between the wheel and the aft locker I was unable see where I was going. To any passing boat (had there been one) it would have seemed that *Fathom* was under the command of a small garden gnome looking in the wrong direction. I was also forever worried the bucket would either collapse under my weight or start sliding slowly across the already cramped space by the wheel before upending itself and me in the scuppers.

I stayed on the helm for another hour or so before deciding that eating something and getting some rest outweighed the risks of Otto being overwhelmed. I switched him on and went below. I rummaged through a couple of lockers looking for nothing in particular but, realising I was too tired to cook anything, crashed out fully-clothed in a heap on the quarter-berth. Although darkness falls quickly at these latitudes, I managed to drag myself back to being awake only 20 minutes later but feeling as if I had slept for twice that long. The wind was moderating to force 5/6 and the seas were reducing so I climbed back into the cockpit, shook a reef out of the main, rigged a preventer on the boom but left three reefs in the genoa.

Whilst under-canvassed for the conditions, *Fathom* was as solid as a rock. I needed some deep sleep during the coming night, with no unpleasant surprises. Before allowing myself that luxury, though, I realised I really did need something to eat. I raided the cool-box and lockers to make myself a mouth-watering Thai green curry, my first proper hot meal in 60 hours. I also allowed myself a cele-bratory small brandy before gratefully returning to the quarter-berth around 22.00hrs. As an added precaution, I turned the radar on and set the alarm to go off if another vessel came within a seven mile radius.

30 Nov – 10:09 GPS – pos: N24°23' | W019°00'

Distance covered in last 24 hours	*167 nm*
CL total	*339 nm*
HL total	*372 nm*
+/–	*–33 nm*

Well, what a difference a good night's rest can make. After very little sleep over the previous couple of days and tired from the concentration needed to hand steer throughout most of yesterday's big seas I badly needed some catch-up sleep. I managed around six hours in short bursts between cockpit and nav station.

The interior of *Fathom* had been well thought out. The sleeping and cabin arrangements were well designed and gave me ample choice depending on conditions. Whilst there was a large master cabin forward of the saloon I realised any seaway would make sleeping there uncomfortable. My sleeping arrangements on *Fathom* for the transat confined themselves to either the saloon quarter berth to port or the U-shaped saloon sofa to starboard depending upon which tack I was on. During the storm I had used both, wedging myself firmly into the starboard berth with cushions to avoid being thrown chin-first into or under the saloon table. My preferred berth was, however, to port in front of the nav station which was stern-facing.

The nav station contained all my principal instruments – an electronic chartplotter showing position, speed, heading, wind strength and direction and other more technical information; radar with a 20 mile radius; VHF radio; fuel, temperature and battery level gauges; a Navtex weather report receiver; an integrated CD/radio and all the electrical switches for the onboard systems. Secured to the bulkhead immediately next to the nav station was one of four on-board dry-powder fire extinguishers and above which, suspended by two bungee cords from the grab-rail running along the saloon roof, hung my two short sea fishing rods fitted with heavy reels, lines and lures. Lying on my back I felt I was in a mix of an electrical hardware store and a small fishing tackle shop. However, from this position I was able to monitor the instruments at the nav station by the foot of my berth without getting up. This was a huge advantage in the first two weeks as my ribs remained pretty sore and made sleeping in any position other than on my back impractical.

The previous night, largely due to the ribs, I woke frequently. As it was, since leaving, sleep periods had tended to be no more than 45 minutes. However, one lasted 90 minutes and was blissful oblivion. Between each I would briefly visit the cockpit or sit at the nav station in the dim lights of the electronic displays to complete the log and to check heading and conditions. I was pleased to find this rhythm increasingly easy to adjust to and sufficiently restful. In the months preceding the trip I had been curious to know how I would adapt to the soloist's interrupted sleep. Several of the books I had read by other solo sailors talked about finding a personal rhythm of being at sea alone. Most suggested it took three to four days, after which the mind and body coalesce. Tony Bullimore described it as when *'the boat and sea start to grow on me. Slowly, I forget the land and the yacht becomes my world. I feel the heartbeat of the hull beneath my feet'*. My first couple of days had been unexpectedly busy but when I got up just before first light around 05.00hrs to put the kettle on I felt much better and relaxed.

With the onset of the bad weather I had almost completely lost my appetite and this had continued for the last 36 hours. I had promised Shaunagh before I left that I would force feed myself if this happened, partially in an effort to make inroads into the absurd amount of supplies crammed onboard. This I had done but with little enthusiasm or enjoyment until the previous evening. But waking now, I still felt hungry. I boiled the kettle, rummaged in the fridge and 15 minutes later, armed with a mug of tea and an entire packet of fried bacon stuffed between two pieces of flabby white bread, went on deck. It was one of the most soul-restoring breakfasts I have ever had as I sat alone in the cockpit watching a spectacular post-storm dawn break over the eastern horizon. There can be few more beautiful *son et lumiere* shows on this planet. For the first time I began to appreciate just what an extraordinary place the ocean was.

Looking at the log, lying a'hull during the storm had put me someway behind my planned schedule. However, with the last 24 hours beam-reaching in winds decreasing from force 7 to force 5 I had covered a very quick 167 nautical miles and recovered much lost ground. It had been a demanding but massively invigorating 24 hour solo run. My only regret is that it had been too rough to see any wildlife and I hoped to start spotting whales, dolphins or turtles at some stage in the rapidly improving conditions.

1 Dec – 14:12 GPS – pos: N22°52' | W020°41'

Distance covered in previous 24 hours	*138 nm*
CL total	*477 nm*
HL total	*492 nm*
+/–	*–15 nm*

The storm was now well past and I was relieved to hear from Shaunagh that all 24 transatlantic rowers had delayed their start for 72 hours until today due to the weather. Having rowed for many years I could not imagine how their much smaller boats, with very low freeboards, could possibly have coped in the conditions I had just been through. It would have been violent, dangerous and exhausting. Shaunagh confirmed that nine people had been killed when Delta hit the Canary Islands and, tragically, no trace was ever found of the boat containing the African immigrants.

Throughout the morning the wind gradually decreased to force 4 and the seas became moderate. I was still tired and took this opportunity to try and appreciate my somewhat abnormal surroundings. Although I knew I was now far offshore and unlikely to be near another boat, I felt very little sense of isolation. The little sense of isolation that did exist, however, gave me feelings of surprising contentment. Never having spent much time on my own I was interested to observe that I felt very at ease and unexpectedly confident in what I was doing. Moving about the boat had stopped being dangerous to life and limb and I felt not unlike someone released after a considerable period of solitary confinement – a peculiar sensation given that was exactly my position. Whilst always clipped on to one of the webbing jackstays running full length down both sides of the deck if going forward, I no longer went stooped, grabbing at every handhold, warily watching each wave and timing each movement. Instead I found a welcome change in going forward and just sitting on the foredeck watching and listening to the watery foam rushing down either side of the hull. It was odd to think of the thousands of feet of water between me and the sea-floor; how many strange animals of all sizes slithered, slid or swam in the blackness where sunlight never penetrates; how many other sailors since time began had been at this exact same spot with the exact same thoughts? My senses seemed to be growing much more acute the further I went offshore and I began to experience a powerful feeling of solitude. This was the first time I began to appreciate the big difference between being alone as opposed to being lonely. It was an unexpected but very welcome realisation.

I had now completed just under 500 nautical miles and was aiming to cross the 20' parallel at 25' of longitude. Part of the reason for this was advice given to the ARC fleet which had left a week ahead of me to stay a minimum 100 miles off the African coastline to avoid the unlikely but potential threat of pirates. This was reinforced for me by a disturbing story I had read in the sailing press the previous year of a yacht being followed at night 125 miles northwest of the Cape Verde Islands. Frustratingly, the wind had backed again to the south west and I had to head either west into light winds or south and close the African coast. As the latter gave me greater speed I could not avoid closing the coastline more than I felt really comfortable.

As a result, I still do not fully know whether what happened next was due to frustration over my position, to accumulated tiredness or just plain fact. However, it was not nice. It was also all too real and for the first time in my life I knew I was frightened.

At about 22.00hrs I came up on deck to make a last check before turning in. It was very dark, the moon not yet up. Taking a quick look around the boat, I was very surprised to see dim lights from another boat. I dropped below and had a quick look on the radar. This confirmed that the other boat was only 2 miles off, not very big but closing quite quickly on a direct course towards me. How big is this part of the Atlantic? As I was only sailing under a small masthead light I reached across the nav desk and flipped on all my navigation lights, assuming they hadn't seen me. Climbing back on deck I watched for some sign of a course alteration. There was none. Going back below I quickly monitored their course on the radar which confirmed they were still heading straight at me. I suddenly felt sick. Knowing I was still less than 100 miles off the Mauritanian coast I doused all my lights, raced up into the cockpit, turned the engine on and dramatically turned 90 degrees to port under my full speed of 8.5 knots. I threw my jacket over the binnacle to put us in total darkness and decided I had no time to do anything with the sails. Trying to ignore flapping sails, avoid the gybing boom and the fact I couldn't see what I was doing only added to my sense of alarm and over-whelming unease. Standing at the wheel and holding my breath I turned to watch for any change in the angle of their lights to indicate they had not followed me. For a moment they held their original course but, after five or six seconds, with an awful feeling in the pit of my stomach, I saw their lights swing slowly onto my new heading in silent pursuit.

I find it very hard to describe my exact feelings at that moment. Words cannot capture that instant when you go from concern to a realisation of very real fear. I felt the blood drain from my face and my mind slowed right down. It was not the same fear that comes from being faced by bad weather or a natural danger. It was a much more basic animal fear – a fear of being hunted. My mind went from bewildered shock to slow motion and seemed to hang in suspended animation and disbelief as I tried to understand what was happening. I found it difficult to focus my thinking on what options I had. Strangely, my immediate thought was not for myself but of Shaunagh and our children. I very briefly wondered whether I should try and call her on the satellite phone but realised it would take too long and only frighten her. Besides, what on earth would I say? My life did not flash in front of my eyes but I did start thinking as to how long I could ward off what now seemed inevitable. I have never before in my life felt so completely impotent and vulnerable. I knew I had to unscramble my brains and force myself to think logically. Taking a couple of deep breaths to get my heart rate down, I desperately tried to think. If they had radar it was only a question of time until I was overhauled. My only hope was that they did not have radar and to try to throw them off my course and make them guess where I was in the pitch black. I decided to throw in a couple more sharp turns and, somehow, try and get behind them. I reasoned that was the least likely place they would think of looking for me.

It also gave me a position from which I could exercise some control by shadowing their movements. To do this, however, meant I was going to have to close the distance between both vessels and pass them down one side.

Over the next minutes I threw in a series of slower turns holding my breath to see what they did. It felt as if each lasted forever as I desperately watched their lights for any sign of a change. I was concentrating so hard on what they were doing that I became completely disorientated as to heading and became quite probably confused myself. I do not recall much of that time but do remember when I suddenly realised the angle of their lights had altered as I started coming round on my track. Rapidly going below to grab my binoculars I raced back on deck and tried to make out shape, size and heading. With no moon it was nearly impossible but, with a surge of adrenalin, I estimated the remaining 500 meters between us was changing rapidly as both boats started to pass one another. I held my breath for a long time as I saw their stern light come abreast of me. If they were going to see me it was now. Feeling desperately tense I reduced my speed to cut down on my bow wave and started a gradual turn to come directly astern. Under a minute later, dropping down the companionway again I checked the radar screen. I was directly behind them. I throttled back further and held my speed at six knots. Slowly, I followed in their wake and gradually, almost imperceptibly at first, the distance between us began to increase. I held their heading and my speed. I had no idea what bearing we were both on. Frankly, so long as the distance continued to grow I was going to hold to it like a condemned man to a royal pardon.

Over the next hour I must have been up and down the companionway a hundred times. Gradually reducing engine speed I allowed the gap to widen. At some stage, I can't remember after how long, the radar showed I was six miles astern and I gradually started to bring *Fathom* back on to our original heading. For the following hour, under autopilot, I sat at the nav station glued to the dull glow of the radar screen watching for any sign of course alteration by them. I was worried that they would guess I had altered back on to my original bearing and would follow in the hope of keeping up with me until dawn came. Two hours later, when the radar showed us 16 miles apart, the echo from the other boat had become faint and there had been no change in their heading. Dawn was still some two to three hours away and whilst I was still not completely confident that the scare was over I gave myself a very large brandy. I also felt very, very tired. The effect of the adrenalin that had pumped throughout my system for the last 4 hours was rapidly wearing off.

Realising that I needed some 'down' time, I set two alarms at 30 minute repeating intervals so as I could continue to check relative radar positions and crashed out fully clothed on the pilot berth. Both alarms did their unpleasant work and twice dredged me back from oblivion to the radar screen. By dawn there was no trace of anything on the horizon or radar screen.

Looking back on those few hours is now rather like remembering snatches of a very bad dream. The whole

thing seems almost surreal. I had never before felt so threatened and vulnerable, not even when running a line for the
Oxford University drag hounds thirty years earlier. When
I had done that, after a 15 minute head start I heard the
huntsman call hounds onto my scent with his horn and
the pursuing pack begin to speak. The realisation I was
their prey had quickened my pulse and running pace but
it was still in good humour. This had altogether been
different. My imagination had gone way beyond being
chased by trained hounds. It had entered realms of real
fear and my sense of vulnerability had been that much
more acute through being alone. Of course, it didn't occur
to me until much later that whoever had followed me
would have been completely unaware that I was alone.
Who were they? What had they wanted? The most likely
explanation is that it was a returning fishing boat and
they had picked up my masthead light and seen I was
moving slowly. Opportunistically, I assume they had hoped
to come alongside quickly and quietly. To what purpose?
The imagination can come up with all kinds of scenarios
from cash and cameras to more aggressive acts. It is not
worth speculating on what never happened. When I picked
up speed and started to zigzag they unquestionably
followed for a while but gave up when they realised their
element of surprise had gone and that I was likely to be
fully crewed. Whatever the cause, whatever the reason, I
was immensely glad it was over. The only question that
plays in my mind now is, why did they keep their navigation lights on?

When dawn arrived the weather, like my mood, was

overcast with drizzle. I tiredly realised the fast beam reaching of the day before would not be repeated as the wind had swung to the east northeast and was down to force 4. As a form of mental therapy to having felt so vulnerable and alone I decided to have another go at retrieving the 34 emails Shaunagh told me had been sent to my inbox and which I seemed unable to access. I suspect the technological obstruction was me but, after only a short while and despite the events of the previous night, I suddenly felt strangely half-hearted about having my new found surroundings and space invaded by updates from friends and family back in air-conditioned offices and the confines of daily domestic life ashore. I felt I was on a very different planet and one which had little relevance to anyone but me.

My mood changed to feeling overwhelmingly tired and I resorted to completing listlessly a variety of small jobs to make myself feel useful. The wind copied my mood and did little all day, giving me my first real experience of being on a remarkably benign ocean. It felt very strange, as if *Fathom* and I were tiptoeing over a slumbering giant. I could hardly believe the change in the weather in only four days.

Over dinner I listened to Michael Palin read extracts from his 'Himalaya' series which helped restore some of my spirits. This especially so when he informed me in sombre tones that one particular bad and depressing day had been made infinitely worse when dinner was finally presented to him in his tent – goat in batter and a tuna sauce. It made me feel so much better when I prepared a plate of smoked salmon and a bowl of slightly burned mushroom goulash.

I never did manage to fix my inbox problem. This proved to be something of a pity as, when I finally got back to London, I spent a very happy couple of hours reading through all the emails I never received. A couple were classics and would have cheered me up immeasurably on a number of occasions when tired. My favourite was from two non-boating wags in my office:

Dear Spino, Rupert and I have been looking at the map on your website and after some debate between ourselves we've decided you are heading in the right direction. Well done!

2 Dec – 11:50 GPS – pos: N21°20' | W022°06'

Distance covered in previous 24 hours	133 nm
CL total	610 nm
HL total	612 nm
+/–	–2 nm

After a fast but, again, disturbed night (a reward for a pretty slow previous day) I woke before dawn to find the first hints of the trades – wind was force 6 and the swell had moved from NW to ENE, the same as the wind. During the night I had twice been on deck, once to reef both main and genoa as the wind started to rise. *Fathom* is fitted with roller-bearing mainsail cars (small attachments to which the mainsail is attached that slide up and down the mainsail track on the mast for raising and lowering the mainsail) and which make taking reefs relatively easy without having to turn into the wind.

Wearing a head-torch I would slack off the main halyard a few feet, wind in the slack on the reefing line and then repeat the process until the reef was fully in. At night, most of this was done by feel but the head torch did help me to see what was happening up the mast when, as sometimes happened, things suddenly seemed to jam. Normally it was one of the battens that had got caught on a spreader or one of the reefing blocks had got twisted but throughout the trip reefing was surprisingly easy even in strong following winds.

This morning, with the overnight reefs still in, I was broad running fast downwind to cross 20′ latitude close to 25′ longitude. This should have put me in the northern section of the trade wind belt. Barbados is at 13′ latitude so I would still have to work my way southwards as well as westwards but I was hopeful that the winds would hold as good as they currently were. For the first time on the trip I was enjoying proper surfing off 4 metre waves at over 8 knots. Fantastic.

Surfing is a wonderful experience. This especially so when alone and in a 12 metre boat under a blue sky with a perfect wind. I did not have the large cruising chute up as the wind direction and strength suited fast sailing under main and genoa. The wind was running at an angle across the wave pattern giving me and *Fathom* the opportunity to set ourselves up properly whilst sailing with the wind but at an angle across the waves. When I had got the sails balanced, I tightened my grip on the wheel and slowly swung it to start a gradual turn to bring the wind onto my quarter and to re-position us to face in the same direction as the waves were running. It felt exactly as if we were coming out of the pit-lanes and onto a race track. As the wind angle began to change, our speed started to increase rapidly and more weight came onto the wheel as boat speed forced the rudder to bite into the water now beginning to race faster under the hull. I widened my grip on the wheel as, with a surge of energy, we moved into top gear and began moving almost as fast as the waves around us. Slowly, a large wave coming from behind started to lift the stern of the boat. I felt myself being inexorably raised into the air and staring down at *Fathom's* bow that was now pointing down the face of the wave as the crest came level with me in the cockpit. Then, to the sound of breaking water, the crest started to boil and we surged forward like a surfboard being pushed on by the pent-up power in the tonnes of water now underneath us. The acceleration was adrenalin pumping as I held the boat straight fighting the pressure that was building on the rudder. For half a minute we surfed the wave shaking and vibrating as the massive body of water first grabbed then pushed us before gradually overtaking to leave us in a foam covered trough to catch our breaths. With white water all around me I had felt almost as if I had been on a huge toboggan on the Cresta run like my father. For a few moments we returned to a more normal sailing speed before, once again, I started to feel the stern begin to rise behind me – the next wave had arrived.

Though requiring strong concentration, I found the surfing and the adrenalin it produced helped shake off some of the tiredness of the last couple of days. After the storm and the anxiety of being followed, last night had started that process. It had been the first time I really felt relaxed enough to sit in the cockpit after sunset and spend a few minutes taking in the sheer scale of my surroundings. Words can't really do justice to the open ocean at any time of day or night. I suspect an endless, all-encircling horizon and the thought of no other human in close proximity is not everyone's idea of fun. I don't think it's an acquired taste and you either feel completely at ease or uncomfortable. Once I had got over the novelty factor, the ocean became an ever-changing environment as the sea and sky changed continually like two powerful siblings playing then arguing in turn. I became the fascinated solo bystander suspended between them in my little isolated part of the ocean, powerless to control their moods but able to take benefit from them. The only time I felt I did not want to be on deck was in the closing minutes of each day as the sun finally dipped under the horizon. This became a feeling that persisted throughout the trip and, most evenings, I went below to shower and cook dinner during sunset and to re-emerge into the cockpit only once darkness had fallen.

By now I had covered 600 miles and was approximately 180 miles off the African coast and entering the immensity of the open ocean. Beneath me the sea floor was rapidly dropping to the abyssal plain at a depth of 16,000 feet, above me the infinity of the night sky went from horizon to horizon. With no man-made light pollution at all it was an extraordinary sight with my two favourite constellations, the Plough and Orion's belt, surrounded by far more stars than I had ever seen before. I lay down on my back along one side of the cockpit and looked up at the inky-black night sky waiting to catch the momentary flash of shooting stars. It fascinated me to think that after a millennium of careering through the vastness of outer space they burned up in seconds as they hurtled through the very edge of the earth's atmosphere. At 6 knots I didn't feel competitive about doing quite the same across the vastness of the open ocean but I did feel strangely re-assured that little in my whole view had changed in the last few millions of years. Previous generations of seafarers from Columbus and Drake to Chichester and Moitessier must have looked up at exactly the same stars and maybe felt the same wonder at the enormity of space and the insignificance of human nature. However, insignificant or not, even here *homo sapiens* has now planted his seed as I noticed amongst the twinkling stars the slow controlled orbit of a satellite, glimmering faintly like a far distant torch, sliding its computerised course through the night sky.

In contrast, the one completely natural event that never ceased to fascinate me was the phosphorescence. After sunset, once the last embers of the day had been finally extinguished, the mood of the ocean often changed from one of restless curiosity to that of utter blackness where all light was sucked from the air like sound in fog. On cloudy nights, until the moon rose over the horizon some hours after sunset, it felt almost as if we had been swallowed and were in the belly of some vast whale. It was then that I would sit on the transom and look down at the phosphorescence being created by the boat's hull moving through that inky blackness. I first noticed it after the seas had flattened out following the storm. Initially, it was intermittent and weak but as I sailed progressively south west it got better and stronger each night. Until a few hundred miles west of the Cape Verde Islands when the phosphorescence disappeared as quickly as it had appeared, I ended up most evenings sitting for half an hour or so in the cockpit watching as each wave was pushed aside by *Fathom's* bows. A cascade of sparkling phosphorescence would tumble across the foaming surface and momentarily look like the mirror image of the starry night sky high above me. The most fascinating aspect was the phosphorescence created by the keel underwater. Looking astern from the cockpit I watched as, every three or four seconds, a bright ball of phosphorescence burst into light like an electric bulb two metres below the surface. Unlike on the surface, these 'bulbs' stayed on for sufficient time to create a short but constant dotted line of two or three such lights in my wake. It was almost as if I was driving in the middle of a country lane along the dotted white lines. It fascinated me for hours and I wondered whether whales and dolphins ever create the same display of natural light for evening family entertainment.

Throughout the day conditions continued to give an invigorating fast run under reefed main and genoa. I was making such good progress that I still didn't consider putting up the cruising chute. Instead I concentrated for really the first time since leaving on getting *Fathom* balanced and sailing as well as she could. I was quite surprised at the level of constant concentration this required. Before I had left the UK my brother, Giles, had come round for supper. He knows me well and we agreed that most of the challenges I would face on the transat could be categorised into three disciplines – physical, technical and mental. All three were required to varying degrees as I set the boat up to make maximum advantage of conditions.

I had confidence in my physical condition. I was 50 years old and had trained properly and hard for 12 months. I felt fitter than at any time since my last boat race for Oxford in 1977. A regular mix of running, cycling and weights three to four times a week had removed two inches off my waist and put an equivalent amount of muscle on my upper body. When I now walked past the bathroom mirror I no longer flinched and, quite often, wandered casually back for a second look. When I jumped up and down bits of me no longer continued going up and down long after the rest of me had stopped. I felt good. Part of this had been achieved in the Covent Garden gym with Jackie, a persistent and very experienced trainer and with whom Shaunagh and I shared laughs, sweat and pain. I took huge pleasure when Jackie told Shaunagh that she considered me way fitter than my age group and a 'leisure athlete'. This I immediately assumed distinguished me from her more normal client struggling with middle age, suit trousers made ten years earlier and with only three weeks before the summer holiday and the embarrassing unveiling of the expense account stomach in front of friends and family. However, I took rather less pleasure when she also suggested that to maintain this distinction I should take up the triathlon.

I was also comfortable with the technical aspect of the transat. After three years sailing *Fathom* I now felt very familiar with her. She was not a racer but a comfortable fast cruiser and one of a limited edition of that particular model fitted with a taller rig. She had shown very good stability and handling on the various trips we had made to Mallorca, Menorca, Sardinia and Corsica during the previous seasons and, from that aspect, she had rapidly been adopted by us all as a family member. Earlier in 2005, when coming back in that storm from Sardinia I had helmed the boat almost continuously throughout taking only short naps. During one of them I had drifted off to an uneasy short sleep with the slightly unnerving sound of hymns being sung in the cockpit by Shaunagh, Harry and Rosie not because they were overly worried *Fathom* would let us down but to keep spirits up. At least it enabled me to see and learn how *Fathom* best handled strong conditions and for Shaunagh to see how I handled the same conditions and lack of sleep. We both passed.

The final discipline of mental preparedness was an unknown one for me. Whilst rowing at international level for five years had demanded the highest level of mental preparation and commitment that had been almost 30 years ago. It had also involved very close continuous interaction with and reliance on other crew members. I had never done anything like this before and certainly never been completely on my own for any meaningful length of time. My brother Giles said he thought I would hate the whole experience without others around me. Uncomfortably too many friends had also put on that awful 'concerned' face, looked deep into my eyes, put their hand on my arm and quietly said 'You're so brave. Won't you be lonely?' To me, bravery is a judgement made by others based on their own reactions to any given situation. I felt perfectly happy with mine but the issue of loneliness did begin to play on my mind increasingly as the departure date loomed. Now, looking back on the whole trip, I can genuinely say that from the moment I cast off I never again thought or worried about loneliness. It never occurred to me. I was alone, but that is an entirely different thing.

3 Dec – 13:00 GPS – pos: N20°37' | W024°23'

Distance covered in previous 24 hours	140 nm
CL total	750 nm
HL total	732 nm
+/–	+18 nm

Well, a rather frustrating night chasing zephyrs. I spent quite a lot of it on the foredeck adjusting runners and looking like a cross between Bob the Builder (harness and safety lines) and Arthur Scargill (torch strapped to head). My Pythonesque worry was not so much losing my footing over the side but being hit in the face by a formation of flying fish attracted to my head-torch. Having one eye that doesn't work properly makes me overly protective about taking a direct hit in the other from airborne sardines.

Actually, flying fish are amongst the finest acrobats

of the oceans and this morning I found my first salted corpse lying on deck. As a child on my father's boat in the Mediterranean, I remember regularly seeing shoals (or should it be flocks?) of flying fish. Sadly that is a very rare sight nowadays, certainly in the western Mediterranean, and so it was that much more exciting to see them once again in vast numbers. Other sailors had told me of coming on deck each morning and regularly finding dead flying fish in the scuppers and which had obviously hurled themselves onto the boat in the darkness. Whether this was from blind pilotage or by being attracted to the dimmed lights on the boat is hard to tell, but virtually every morning for the first two weeks I had to pick up two or three on my morning inspection around the deck. Those that flew alongside the boat gave me ceaseless pleasure in watching their frantic flight, bouncing and accelerating off waves mid-flight to moisten their wings and to gain more height and distance. Some travelled extraordinary distances of up to 200 metres at speed before crashing, head first, into the side of a wave and disappearing as quickly as they had appeared. It was amazing to think how quickly they must retract their delicate translucent wings to avoid damaging them. Whilst none that landed on the deck were big enough to cook, the large ones are delicious to eat as I later discovered.

Since dawn and removing the small, stiff and salted corpse of my nocturnal flying visitor I had a frustrating hour sitting on the foredeck trying unsuccessfully to get the chute up. This was my first solo effort to do so on the trip. I had experimented successfully a number of times on my own earlier in the summer but with crew on hand if needed. However, after a depressingly short time, it seemed to me that the whole process was fraught with enough reasons for leaving it well alone. The main problem was that I had rigged the removable inner forestay on leaving Las Palmas and I felt it could now interfere with hoisting the chute. I wanted to remove it before trying again. Truth be told, I was probably just apprehensive about hoisting the chute completely on my own as they are big sails, pack a powerful punch and I had to avoid getting a wrap. This is when the long sock in which the chute is hoisted, as if in a sausage skin, is slid up, releasing the 450 square feet of light Dacron which then starts wildly flapping around in the air until brought under control. This is normally done by another crew member back in the cockpit. Without that extra pair of hands the chute would flap around noisily and violently until I had scrambled back to the cockpit and tightened up the lines. It was during this scramble back to the cockpit that the chute could potentially wrap itself around the forestay and damage itself or get stuck around the genoa. Either would cause a problem and calm and controlled speed by me would be essential.

As it was, I spent a fruitless 20 minutes dragging the bagged chute onto the foredeck and crawling back and forth, sorting out the order in which everything needed to be done. This achieved, I sat on the foredeck looking up the mast thinking how high the top looked. I then looked at the chute lying in its sausage curled like a snake all around me on the deck and thought how much there was of it. It was one of those 'bugger, there's a lot that can go wrong' moments and I lost my nerve. I decided to play safe and delay a chute hoist on the basis that I needed to remove the inner forestay first. I decided to do that after lunch. The good thing about having tried is at least I had reminded myself that the art of solo sailing depends heavily on the three 'Ps' of Planning, Preparation and Procedure. Unable to rely on anyone else makes solo sailing that much more important to get it right first time. When things go wrong, most sailors will find the three 'Ps' replaced by the single 'F'.

I planned to turn more westward shortly to cross 20^0 latitude, some 750 miles after leaving the Canaries. I was hoping that would give me a better wind angle for the chute and more consistent speed after the very mixed last few days. I was also starting to keep an eye on my diesel levels as both running the generator to recharge the batteries for the autopilot and trying to get out of Delta's path had burned more than expected. I was already beginning to worry that the last 48 hours run into Barbados would need to be all manual. Thank goodness Malcolm and the boys had bought extra diesel jerry-cans on their delivery run. These were now stowed, full, in the cockpit locker.

4 Dec – 10:03 GPS – pos: N19°46' | W025°17'

Distance covered in previous 24 hours	*86 nm*
CL total	*836 nm*
HL total	*852 nm*
+/−	*−16 nm*

Last night, unusually, I sat in the cockpit and watched a wonderful sunset and became quite lost in all the colours. This was probably largely the fault of a badly needed chilled can of beer on a rather empty stomach. With the weather so far having required bouts of extended concentration, I had been cautious in my approach to drinks other than water. My only non-essential experiment to date had been one of the 30 high-energy fruit supplements Shaunagh had insisted I take and which was easily the single most unpleasant experience of the entire trip. As far as alcohol was concerned, in all my pre-planning I had held a lengthy debate with myself over whether or not to have any on-board. Bit of a silly debate really as I always knew the answer would be a cautious yes. Any lingering doubt was certainly removed when Cathy and Kenneth gave me the most superb bottle of cognac as an essential 'survival aid'. How could I seriously have declined such a gift? They both run endless marathons and physically demanding events such as the Marathon des Sables and the Atacama Crossing. If that wasn't enough to make me feel my trip was no more than a walk in the park, they complete all their events dressed in large rubber theatrical Rhino suits as Cathy runs Save the Rhino in England. The final decider for me was that Kenneth has an encyclopaedic knowledge of Highland single malts. I could only assume this came from a wide and in-depth practical study of the subject matter and as he is as fit as a butcher's dog I didn't see any reason why I couldn't likewise indulge.

Having said all that, however, I studiously limited myself to a maximum of two small cans of beer during the day and, subject to the weather, to restrict any wine to supper. On a number of days I had touched neither. Given I was by now far enough south to be drinking four to five litres of water a day, I thought this an acceptable approach. The self-imposed restriction on the wine had resulted from my 48 hour solo three months earlier from Spain to Sardinia. On that trip I purposefully only allowed myself a limited number of 20 minute catnaps during the two nights afloat to monitor my response to a number of issues. One had been alcohol and it was interesting to discover that very limited beer consumption had no discernable effect on me whilst one glass of red wine had been more effective than the most powerful sleeping pill. On that occasion I had slung two kitchen timers around my neck set at 20 and 30 minute intervals to make certain I woke up again. Brutal but effective. Interestingly, spirits were somewhere between the two (albeit outside of the occasional brandy or even rarer whisky I really don't like spirits much). I also battled briefly with the perception that many seem to have that drinking on your own must be the sign of a closet alcoholic. This is not something I readily understand. To me, it either suggests such people can't trust themselves to stop before falling over or that they only drink when amongst others for confidence. I love wine and am happy to spoil myself rotten with or without support. Being on my own I took a firm view, however, that any form of alcohol should only be seen as genuinely medicinal or a reward for a good day and then only if conditions were favourable.

On that basis, the drinks locker had remained almost

completely undisturbed for the last week as conditions had pre-occupied me more than the thought of a drink. Last night, as the wind had nearly died and the seas were almost flat I uncorked a bottle of wine and spoiled myself with a nip of cognac as well. I was hoping the combination would help me relax and catch up on some lost sleep.

No such luck. This morning, after a second night requiring constant visits to the cockpit to trim the sails in very light conditions, all wind finally disappeared. I was making 0.34 knots in 3 knots of breeze on a SW heading. Since 19.00hrs last night I had only made 30 miles. It was looking like a long 24 hours!

Over the last couple of days it had become noticeably warmer, especially within minutes of sunrise. The temperature difference either side of dawn was striking. Normally, almost as soon as I had got up, I would sit in the cockpit nursing a steaming mug of black coffee. In the dark of pre-dawn it was cool enough to need a sailing fleece as I sat perched in my favourite corner of the cockpit under the spray-hood looking aft, absorbing what the boat was telling me about the wind and water. As the tip of the sun appeared over the horizon, bleaching the multi-coloured first flush of dawn, air temperatures rose with it. By the time the sun was fully over the horizon, a matter of minutes, the fleece became obsolete. As the sun rose higher throughout the morning, my other clothes were discarded one by one until by midday I ended up behind the wheel looking like a large plucked turkey with only a harness around my chest.

Around midday, especially on days when the winds

were light and even though I had a bimini for shade, I often found myself checking the water temperature display on the instrument panel. Under other circumstances I may have lowered the stern ladder and climbed down into the water to be pulled along through the cooling ocean waters. Shaunagh had often done this when on passage mid-Mediterranean, once even diving overboard when we were under full sail as she had spotted whales surfacing nearby. On that occasion I also had two tuna lines trailing behind the boat with large submerged hooks and I had struggled to get lines in, sails down, keep track of where she was and both boat and temper under control. She had almost given me a terminal heart attack, which would have served her right. However, being solo now gave me neurotic visions of the ladder bracket suddenly breaking free, a gust of wind making me lose my grip or a completely irrational fear of the three miles of water directly beneath me. In his memoirs my father writes of the same feelings and goes on to say:

'We did not often bathe in mid-ocean. One does not know what creature may not have joined the train. But on the occasions we did, we noted a curious vertiginous effect. As one peered down through the water below, where sunbeams refracted through the surface, glittered down as they fell to their death a few hundred metres below, one became giddy at the thought that the bottom was many thousands of metres below that. Only a very slightly greater buoyancy kept you from falling down through the blue void and a panic froze one that it might suddenly cease to do so.'

In 23 days, no matter how warm it got, I didn't so much as even dangle my feet off the stern.

In the slow conditions experienced today I just looked forward to a less demanding cool shower before supper.

On the plus side, at around 17.00hrs I was visited by a large pod of whales – about 15 in total and probably pilot whales with very bulbous heads. They came to within 100 metres of the boat and whilst I got some photos they were too far away to be able to see much detail. I was grateful Shaunagh was not on board given her predilection for trying to inspect whales at closer quarters.

Dec – 10:21 GPS – pos: N19°17' | W026°52'

Distance covered in previous 24 hours	97 nm
CL total	933 nm
HL total	972 nm
+/-	–39 nm

I NEED MORE WIND!

Two sub-100 mile days and two consecutive nights of little sleep with seemingly endless trips to the cockpit tweaking sails in light winds. My sleep on each night had been only just over four hours and in short bursts anyway so I could have done without even lower numbers. In the last two nights I hadn't slept for any period exceeding 75 minutes, with most under the hour. However, whilst tired I was surprised and interested not to feel worse, as the weather was increasingly warm and humid. Because of this, I was drinking 5 litres of water during the day and probably another during the night to keep hydrated.

I was curious to observe my mental state in these conditions, which were relaxingly quiet but utterly frustrating and I realised that there was a very noticeable correlation between my moods and the strength of wind. Beaufort may well have been the person whose name was given to different wind strengths but no-one yet appears to have provided a parallel scale for the related impact on the human senses. There is no doubting that for me there was an inverse reaction between wind and frustration – low wind speeds/high levels of frustration and high wind speeds/low levels of frustration. With the former there was no pressure on the sails to keep them full and with even a slight swell the sails slapped, banged and flopped from side to side, damaging both themselves and my mental state. This was when small things could go wrong and one morning, after an endless night of the rig being battered by the flapping and windless sails, I found the shackle pin had detached from the third reefing block and both were lying on the deck. This despite progressively reefing throughout the night to reduce the flapping and a daily inspection of all such pins and shackles. Additionally, quite often there was no discernible forward progress at all. This left me slumped in the cockpit staring over the stern or up at the sky desperately searching for wind like a drunk for alcohol. My recollection of a couple of times when I was becalmed are almost more vivid than others when I was sailing right on the edge of control but with acute concentration. For some reason I felt more vulnerable when becalmed.

This morning was better and with a relatively flat sea I was covering more ground than I had managed at any time during the previous 48 hours.

My other good news was catching two fish for dinner. Up until today conditions had either been too rough for fishing or I had simply not felt bothered. Sitting in the cockpit just after lunch I had seen quite a few flying fish leap out of the water and then, close behind, two fast-moving larger fish in pursuit. The sight of what I thought were two perfect sized tuna of around 5-6 kilos galvanised me into action and I rapidly slipped both lures off the rods in their rod-holders either side of the cockpit and watched as they invitingly skimmed and bounced along the surface 35 metres behind the boat. After only a couple of minutes the tips of both rods suddenly dipped hard and line was stripped off the whirling reels as both lures were taken by unseen predators. We weren't sailing fast enough to need taking a sail down to reel both in and, within a couple of minutes, both were in a bucket. Neither turned out to be particularly large, around 2 kilos each, and were somewhat disappointingly dorados rather than tuna. However, filleted quickly they were delicious later that evening fried in our own home-grown olive oil from Torre Ronsat in Catalunya. I was actually quite glad they were modest in size as, having previously caught two 20 kilo tuna off the boat in the Mediterranean I have no idea what I would have done with the 20 steaks such a large tuna would have produced.

Tonight I ticked off the first 1,000 miles. It was now also under 2,000 miles to Barbados in a straight line.

How close I could stick to that line remained to be seen. However, for the Cazenove sweepstake I estimated that the market in days had come in to 20–23.

6 Dec – 08:24 GPS – pos: N18°52′ | W028°54′

Distance covered in previous 24 hours	125 nm
CL total	1,058 nm
HL total	1,092 nm
+/–	–34 nm

After yesterday morning's very light winds we finally got some decent north easterlies around lunchtime. Taking a firm grip on myself I decided it was now or never to get the chute up for the first time. I dragged the sail-bag out of the locker, clipped onto the jackstays and slowly half-crawled along the side decks pulling the whole lot forward. Once there, I sat on the foredeck and methodically worked out the order of events and the actions each entailed. I lay the sheets along either side of the deck from cockpit to stem-head, pulled the chute still encased in its sausage out of the sail bag, clipped the halyard on and then, trying to ignore my slight apprehension, started to raise the sausage arm over arm whilst sitting at the bottom of the mast. Normally there would be someone in the cockpit to haul in the halyard whilst the sausage was gradually released from the sailbag by a second crew at the mast. Being on my own I had to fill both roles which meant that once the sausage was raised to the top of the mast, I had 17 metres of sausage flopping around from the masthead and 17 metres of loose halyard lying all over the foredeck at my feet. At that stage, quickly and calmly, I had to push the taut end of the halyard into an open jammer at the bottom of the mast to keep the sausage up then slither back into the cockpit to pull in all the slack and lock it off properly on one of the main jammers. It was only then that the sausage was held safely and securely, unable to be blown or fall down and go over the side. That would be a potential disaster.

Still in the cockpit, the next step was to rig and tension the appropriate sheet on a winch. This was the most delicate part of the whole operation as too much tension could trigger the sausage cover to be released prematurely whilst too little would result potentially in a wrap around the forestay when the sausage cover was hauled aloft to release the sail. That too would be a potential disaster.

It's worth pointing out that most of this was taking place on a pitching deck in a 6–12ft sea and with a wind speed of normally 15–20 knots. Bearing in mind the number of different moves required for the whole operation, I clipped and unclipped myself numerous times between cockpit and foredeck. And that was just putting the chute up. I wouldn't have minded quite so much had my lifeline and jackstay not found one another almost completely incompatible and jam continually at the most unexpected and inconvenient moments. This was inevitably midway between cockpit and foredeck when I needed quickly but calmly to make some sail adjustment and the lifeline was trailing between my legs. On each such occasion, as I moved swiftly but carefully along the side-decks towards the cockpit I would be brought to a shuddering halt by a jam causing a sudden explosion of pain in the trouser department. It somewhat raised my apprehension levels each time I raised or lowered the chute.

Finally, all was ready. The sausage was aloft, the lines were rigged and it was time for the release. Going forward I sat right at the bows and, taking a deep breath, pulled hard on the up-haul line that slid the sausage cover (the 'snuffer') up towards the masthead to unleash the beast. After the first ten feet or so, once the wind had started to catch the emerging 450 square feet of Dacron, it was important to retain control of the up-haul. If not concentrating enough, the wind would pull the sail out so fast the line could cause bad rope burn to my hands. Cautiously, once the sausage cover had slid fully up to release the sail, the up-haul then had to be tied off at deck level before I desperately quickly clambered back down the side deck muttering 'please don't warp, please don't', jumped into the cockpit and winched in the sheet to set the sail properly. At that stage the boat would accelerate like a whippet from a box and, subject to wind and sea state, take off for an adrenalin-pumping ride.

And, I'm happy to say, that's what happened most of the time.

Taking it down was marginally less stressful other than the initial slackening of the sheet so that I could go forward to pull down the sausage cover and snuff the sail. On the first couple of attempts I misjudged the full amount and let out too little. I then found myself having a desperate tug-of-war on the bows with me trying to snuff the sail whilst the wind did its best to keep it fully inflated. With my hand wrapped around the snuffer line hanging down from near the masthead I fought not to be pulled aloft or over the side of the boat and had awful visions of being lifted off my feet (or bottom) like a nautical Mary Poppins if a strong gust had hit the boat. I jammed my feet under the guard rails, cursed, hauled and pulled with all my weight, refusing to let go until the beast was snuffed. Twice this foredeck battle ensued, both for some minutes, before I learned the correct amount of line to let out to avoid such a fight.

As dusk fell I took the chute down, raised the main and genoa and, with the wind holding around 20 knots north-easterly, continued surfing at over 8 knots. I contemplated staying up through much of the night to capitalise but, after the last two nights of zephyr chasing, I was just too tired. After the sun had set, I shortened sail and got my head down for the best night's sleep of the trip – seven hours, including one uninterrupted two hour period of deep sleep, the longest so far. *Fathom* appears to have sailed herself majestically all night dropping below 5 knots only just before dawn. One of the reasons for wanting to 'bank' some sleep hours was the forecast. Somewhat worryingly, another tropical storm was developing to my north. It was expected to move southwards over the next two days. By Thursday the forecast was for the centre of the storm to have reached 23´N, only some 300 miles from my current position. So long as it came no further south, all I should expect was 24 hours of headwinds and some level of storm surge. Whilst boring, uncomfortable and likely to slow our progress, I did not expect either to be anywhere near the same level as Delta last week. However, not only did it seem prudent to grab sleep when offered but yesterday I also tacked onto a more southerly course to get more distance between myself and 23´N. I planned to speak with AWC in London over the following 48 hours to monitor the storm's track.

7 Dec – 08:16 GPS – pos: N18°31' | W031°05'

Distance covered in previous 24 hours	*135 nm*
CL total	*1,193 nm*
HL total	*1,212 nm*
+/–	*–19 nm*

With the deep low pressure system to my north starting to move northeast the winds became fluky and veered from NE to E before becoming SE. At 04.00hrs I gybed onto port tack and held a pretty good course direct for Barbados 1,677 miles away. At first light I put a call through to AWC and was concerned to hear the low pressure system, Tropical Storm Zeta, had been up-rated to a hurricane. Just my luck. This year was proving to be one of the worst on record for hurricanes and late storms. Going on deck I could see wisps of high cirrus overhead with thicker cloud behind. As with Delta, I decided to maintain more of a southerly course for the immediate future.

During the morning the cloud began to thicken accompanied by a gradual increase in wind strength. This gave me some of the best sailing so far – beam reaching with Barbados on the nose at quite fancy speeds. As lunch approached I was in the cockpit thinking of what I was going to eat when, turning round to get a bucket, I almost fell over. Appearing just over the horizon and tracking slowly across my course was another sail boat. As I was close to the halfway mark and was about as far from land as could be I found this something of an event as I has seen no sign of another human being for a week. Struggling to put some shorts on (my closest nautical equivalent to Black Tie), I repeatedly called them on the radio but to no effect. Two hours later, as they drew level about 200 metres to port, three blokes appeared standing on their side deck and we all waved frantically at one another and took endless photographs as if it was a Saturday on the Solent. I noticed they were flying the tricolour and, though they had not answered my radio call, I assumed they were French. This impression was somewhat naturally reinforced when I raised my binoculars and got an eyeful of slightly more Frenchman than I was expecting – all were 'au naturel' and jumping up and down with hands and other things waving rather too energetically. Putting my glasses down, I smiled, waved and gybed under their stern shouting 'vive le sport'. As I passed astern, I saw a motif on their quarter and which looked like an ARC insignia. Given their heading I guessed they were en-route to Antigua after making a stop-over in the Cape Verde Islands. It had been a nice surprise but I was still grateful to be on my own. I was also grateful not to be on their heading as, with all their sails up and boomed out, they were rolling quite badly in the lumpy swell. My heading was only slightly more southing in it but that made all the difference.

Once I had watched them disappear over the far horizon in front of me and to bring my mind back to my own little world I opened the first of my big envelopes from Shaunagh. I should explain – just as I cast off in Las Palmas, Shaunagh handed to me a bulging purple plastic carrier bag. Somewhat preoccupied with other things I briefly asked what it was, to which the answer was 'your advent calendar'. Absently I put it in the saloon where it stayed for the first few days, until the storm passed and natural curiosity reminded me of it. Years ago, when we first started going out, I was living on my own in Zurich, and Shaunagh would come out for the occasional weekend. After each such visit I would find little notes and heart-shaped chocolates all around my apartment. Every time I opened drawers, tidied up books and magazines or got cooking pans out of cupboards I would find these little reminders of her tucked away. It was a miracle I never set the apartment on fire by lighting the grill before discovering a short letter put under it. Over the years it had become very much a signature of hers and one which has meant a lot to me at various moments in my life. The purple plastic bag was no exception – in it there were 20 normal sized envelopes and 5 large ones. As with Advent calendars, they were numbered 1–25 but with the large ones being every fifth number. Being a couple of days behind on my paperwork, I had so far opened only 4 of the smaller envelopes. Each had contained a poem and some photos on a different theme (one of the children, our home in Spain, our previous house in Ireland etc) and a rather risqué postcard from Agent Provocateur, all of which had brought a broad smile to my face. Today it was time to open the first of the large envelopes.

Bearing in mind the Christmas theme normally associated with Advent calendars, I was curious as to its contents. Shaunagh is not very religious but all the same I must admit to some surprise when Big'n Busty's Miss November appeared from inside the envelope. It took me a while to adjust my expectations for a jolly, rotund and overdressed Santa to be replaced by a voluminously endowed girl scantily dressed and pouting at me from inside a shower cubicle. That was just the front cover. The rest seemed more associated with an uncooked Christmas turkey than anything else – large pimples and certainly no feathers.

I was reminded that I had two chicken breasts in the fridge for dinner. I went below to call Shaunagh and thank her.

Mood swings occur quickly when tired. Having laughed loudly over my Advent calendar, when I got through to Shaunagh I hit the very lowest point on the trip. She told me I had completely missed my daughter Rosie's 17th birthday yesterday. I felt completely gutted. For a parent to make such a fundamental mistake is bad enough but being in the middle of the ocean and tired really sharpened the guilt and feelings of complete inadequacy. If that wasn't enough, Shaunagh told me that Rosie had not received a single birthday card from anyone nor even an email. For a long while after we had finished speaking I sat in the cockpit in silence holding the lifeless phone in my hands. I felt useless as a parent, very distant from Rosie and very low. I had been selfish enough doing this trip and upsetting those closest to me by going solo. Now I had gone one worse and forgotten something that should be at the core of being a father. The fact my father had never once remembered my birthday (which was exactly one week after his) was immaterial. I, me, Crispin, Rosie's father had forgotten her birthday. My emotions were surprisingly overwhelming to the point that I became angry with Shaunagh for telling me. Why tell me when she knew there was nothing I could do about it? At a complete loss as to how to make amends I quickly decided to call Rosie on the satellite phone but, after dialling her mobile number, only got her answer phone. At least I could hear her voice and was able to leave a message so she could hear mine. That made me feel marginally better and got the brain back to work. I decided to post an immediate plea on my website:

Happy Birthday Rosie . . . for yesterday! What a howler. However, as I can't send a card then this message will have to do and if all those that read this can email happy birthday to her even if you don't know her – she's wonderful (at rmoneycoutts@stowe.co.uk) I would be most grateful as an absent parent.

I had not counted on how many people were logging on to my daily blogs. The following day, when Rosie opened her email to check her inbox, she had 38 new emails. I'm not sure it achieved quite what I was hoping as it made the Stowe School system crash and caused Rosie all sorts of unexpected extra work as she felt she had to answer each email. Various middle-aged friends of mine even mistakenly took that as a sign to try and start an email correspondence with her but at least it will be a birthday I hope she remembers, albeit for many of the wrong reasons.

8 Dec – 08:49 GPS – pos: N17°55' | W033°24'

Distance covered in previous 24 hours	143 nm
CL total	1,336 nm
HL total	1,332 nm
+/–	+4 nm

This morning I called AWC and was told that over the last 12 hours Zeta had been down-rated from hurricane to tropical storm. They also confirmed that it had veered north and away from me. I was very relieved and was left coping with damp, overcast and humid conditions with a sloppy swell. The rowers had all been re-routed along pretty much the same track as mine to avoid any debris the storm may have left over to our north.

Overnight I had slowed somewhat which left me with a 24 hour run of around 135 miles. This was acceptable but AWC told me that the winds were expected to be light for the next couple of days and unlikely to increase much until I had gained more mileage to the southwest. It was very frustrating to be almost at the geographical half way stage 800 miles off the African coast and 1,500 miles to Barbados but still without any established trade winds. These unusual conditions had kept me behind my planned schedule and, whilst I had not used the engine at all after being followed, I was running the generator 2 hours every day to recharge batteries and was beginning to have slight concerns over my diesel supplies. I had also started to wonder if I had an electrical problem.

This had become a real concern this morning when I had woken before dawn and found Otto not working and all my lights dimmed to almost nothing. I instantly realised the batteries were virtually dead. Although my service batteries are separated from my engine battery, I was still galvanised into frantic action in the fear that some electrical disaster had happened. Leaping off my berth I was in the cockpit in five strides and punching the engine start button with my heart in my mouth. With an instantly reassuring 'brrrrrmmmm' VP started first time and the lights immediately flickered once and then returned to full power. My relief was tangible and I kept the engine on for the next two hours for a full charge.

I had fitted a diesel generator a couple of months before leaving Spain knowing I would have relatively high electrical consumption on the transat running the autopilot, nav lights, nav equipment, radar (from time to time) and the fridge. It was designed to produce 6kw and have ample power to keep my three main service batteries charged. However, since leaving Las Palmas the batteries were not effectively holding their charge even after running the generator for two hours. Initially I thought I was not running the generator for long enough but after the first couple of days suspected it was more than that. I am not a great electrician and this was the one area of solo sailing that I realised could become an issue if I experienced problems. It didn't help to have the battery bank located in the bottom of the main cockpit locker under a mountain of inflatable dinghy, spare sails, buckets warps and other nautical paraphernalia. To conserve power I started to restrict myself on all lights and electrical equipment to bare essentials. Whilst this helped, it was marginal and the batteries continued to drain unusually quickly. Something was wrong.

This was a touch unnerving given I was reliant on my electronics for the autopilot at night and the chartplotter for principal navigation. Without Otto I would have to helm manually for extended periods and try to balance *Fathom* when I tried to sleep. Theoretically this is done by trimming both the headsail and foresail to counter-balance one another so that the boat goes in a straight line. In practice I knew it was never so easy. Navigation was less of an issue as I did have two back-up handheld GPS. Before leaving I had also bought a sextant but not had the time to do more than open the box and hold it. I had absolutely no idea how to use it. My father had only ever used a sextant for navigation and I had always wanted to do likewise. I had rather airily (and wrongly) assumed this would be one of the skills I would be able to teach myself in the endless hours of bored inactivity I had initially imagined a solo transat generated – an impression created for me by my father's comments on long distance solo sailing. I can only think he must have been thinking of something entirely different. I might, nonetheless, have tried had the sextant not rather unhelpfully shed a couple of pieces when first removed from the box. Even in one piece it had looked fiercely complex but in three looked impossible. All I could do was to keep a close eye on generator and battery levels.

I envied my father's technical skills. Jinty, my step-mother, always maintained that he was more interested in the navigational and mechanical aspects of sailing whilst I seemed to be driven more by being at sea and sailing. His writings of his transat are littered with references to his endless fiddling with the radio to stave off boredom. I remember once in Majorca, shortly after he first arrived there in 1967, he made a radio test from *Heliousa* moored off our rented house in Alcudia Bay to the UK. His call was interrupted by the Captain of the *Queen Mary*, at that time the largest cruise liner in the world, speaking to Solent Coastguard on his approach into Southampton. I was dead impressed. My father was furious. He sat fuming in his 39ft boat with just me, unable to resume his radio call, as priority was given to the 975ft leviathan easing her way into harbour with a full complement of 2,300 crew and passengers. Member of the Royal Yacht Squadron he may have been but not one with much of a sense of humour.

Concerned with electrical problems, my sense of humour was not particularly apparent at this stage either. It was lowered even further when, whilst tidying the cockpit before turning in, I noticed distant flashes ahead of me. The night sky was partially obscured by cloud but in the available moonlight I could just make out the darkened outline of bulky cumulus some 15 to 20 miles ahead of me. Every 30 seconds or so there were a series of rapid but silent flashes from within the cloud mass, suggesting a large body of unstable air dead ahead of me. I sat down in the corner of the cockpit and for a long while tried to measure my course against the flashes as, not having a lightning conductor, I had always worried about being caught in an electrical storm. I had read too many alarming stories beloved by modern-day nautical publishers of boats being hit by lightning and losing all electronics or, worse, turning over as keel bolts sheered off. As I was almost as far from any land as possible I felt this was not the time or place to provide even more material for such disaster best-sellers. Going below I put one of my hand-held GPS in the microwave. This is not as mad as it sounds. I had read a theory in some sailing magazine that the internal steel cage of a microwave or oven acts as a Faraday cage and protects the delicate electronics within a GPS in the event of a lightening strike. Having double-checked that the timer on the microwave was off, I then went back on deck and clambered along the foredeck to rig a short length of chain from one of the portside shrouds into the sea as a form of earth. Frankly, I was highly sceptical that either would work if we were hit but could think of no other options.

Feeling slightly uneasy, I went below to cook and eat dinner. As I washed up I remember feeling that the air had become much more humid over the last few hours to the point I almost decided to have another shower. However, I decided to conserve water so only brushed my teeth before undressing and lying on the quarter-berth under a light blanket. For a while I strained my ears for sounds of distant thunder but, finally, must have drifted off to an uneasy sleep

9 Dec – 13:11 GPS – pos: N17°24' | W035°50'

Distance covered in previous 24 hours	136 nm
CL total	1,472 nm
HL total	1,452 nm
+/–	+20 nm

Other than the hourly visits to the nav station and cockpit the night remained sticky but uneventful. I 'woke' around 04.30. Looking through the cockpit hatch from my berth I could see that the sky was devoid of any stars and so must have completely clouded over. Overnight there had been no sound or sight of any lightning and I was relieved that we had sailed undisturbed under reefed genoa and main. For a while I lay on my berth in the dull glow of the chartplotter listening to the boat and thinking of interesting topics for my daily blog on the website. From the various instrument panels on the bulkhead I could see that *Fathom* was making just under six knots in a gusting 15 knots of wind and a relatively calm sea. I listened to the water running along the outside of the hull by my head and the occasional creak as a stronger gust made her heel and put more tension on the rig. Everything seemed to be no different to most of the recent pre-dawns I had experienced to date.

Pulling myself slowly up I dressed, brushed my teeth

and put the kettle on. Just as I sleepily poured the hot water onto the coffee and sugar in my mug I heard the sound of what I thought was rushing water quickly followed by a vibration in the hull that started slowly but then rapidly intensified. I remember my brain being very slow to respond but glancing at the anemometer I watched in fascination as the wind indicator started, slowly at first, to accelerate dramatically from 14 knots to 41 knots in about 30 seconds. As the wind started to shriek through the over-canvassed rigging it was almost drowned out by the sound of rain, tons of it, suddenly smashing down in a waterfall from the black and unseen sky. The noise was deafening. Within seconds *Fathom* was shaking violently as wind tore at the wildly flapping sails and sheets flogged against the spray-hood, deck and rigging. I had to get on deck to reduce sail. It was then that one of the oddest things of the trip happened to me; I couldn't decide what to do with my wonderful mug of coffee. With masterful indecision I started to put it in the sink but decided it would fall over – the wind outside was now howling – I tried sipping it but it was far too hot – still the wind howled – I thought of taking it on deck but one look at the deluged and half submerged cockpit dispelled that idea – the wind and rain crashed around us. Finally, realising the boat was taking a battering I wedged the mug carefully in the corner of the sink, raced half-stumbling up the companionway into the cockpit. In the driving rain I winched the genoa fully in and hardened the main on the preventer. The wind was so bad and the scene so black that I could neither see nor hear fully what I was doing and had to feel the last few metres on the furling line. As soon as the genoa was in, *Fathom* weather-cocked into the wind and the shaking subsided substantially.

Unable to do much else, I slid back down the companionway. Soaked, I grabbed my mug from the sink and quickly finished it as the rapidly growing puddle around my feet ran in all directions across the floorboards. To stop myself doing likewise, I braced myself as *Fathom* pitched and rolled violently with the wind buffeting us from all directions in the utter blackness outside. Whatever we had sailed into was distinctly unfriendly.

Ten minutes later, as quickly as they had appeared, both the wind and rain suddenly and utterly disappeared. I was left in an eerie silence. Climbing back into the dripping cockpit I could still see very little but I could just make out the outline of something black and massive just behind me. It was difficult to see clearly but it seemed to stretch both horizontally and vertically above me like a vast gaping black hole. I sat in the cockpit, becalmed but unsure of my surroundings. For the next hour I watched with growing apprehension as the cold light of dawn slowly unveiled a simply massive body of black and dark grey about half a mile astern sitting on the water and spread across a two mile horizon. The main mass appeared to be off to port and I realised that what I had sailed through was merely the very edge of whatever this was. Thank God I had avoided going closer to its centre.

For another hour or so, as watery daylight began filtering down through the humid mist and cloud, I sat hoping that some wind would appear to enable me to get far away from where I was. Any such hopes were extinguished brutally when at last there was enough light and I could see my surroundings more clearly. Spread around me in a semi-circle were three huge, massive, monstrous squalls each a mile or two wide and seemingly as high. In truth, I couldn't actually see their tops and was mesmerised by their scale and colour. Each was a mixture of grey, dark brown and then black as they descended into the ocean. It was impossible to see where the cloud finished and the rain started or where the rain stopped and the ocean started. It was one great black mass from several thousand feet up and I watched as the upper levels of the cloud walls were pushed and pulled by the wind moving them like blackened lungs. I had skirted the one behind me but the other two were spread across my horizon and drifting down on me. The worst thing was that these masses appeared to have sucked all the wind into themselves leaving me becalmed and drifting helplessly. I felt uncomfortably vulnerable and, for the first time, peculiarly unsure what to do.

I decided to call AWC on the satellite phone. They should be able to give me their latest forecast and any other information relevant to my position. I called Simon and, after giving my latitude and longitude (17′ 26N 035′24W), I called back 10 minutes later to be told I had sailed into the edge of the Inter Tropical Convergence Zone (ITCZ) which had drifted much further north than normal. On the satellite photographs he said they could clearly see some of the clouds topping out at 25,000 feet and suggested that it would be best if I could work my way out from where I was. Nice thought.

Throughout the morning I drifted, every now and then catching a brief gust of wind that helped me edge across the oncoming cliff-face of the next mass. The air felt very still and the sea was a peculiar grey with only a very slight swell. It felt oppressive. As the cloud mass closed on me I could see through the binoculars that the sea was quite disturbed a short distance in front of the base or at least what I thought was the base – everything was so pitch black that I had to guess where it started even though it was now almost midday. I decided the best approach was to hoist sufficient sail to deal with winds to force 6 and wait to pick up the winds running across the face of what was clearly almost a wall of solid water falling from the base of the cloud. At that stage I hoped, rather like a surfer, to sail as fast as I could across the face before being overtaken by the body of the mass and sucked into it with too much sail up. Rather a basic theory and requiring a steady head but certainly achievable at the right speed. I set *Fathom* up and returned to the cockpit. Anxiously, I felt as if I was waiting to go over a waterfall rather than through one. Over the next hour, the nearest squall closed on me inexorably. If anything the wind dropped even further until, suddenly and with the cloud base almost on top of us, the wind started to rise rapidly. Almost instantly it went from nothing to 25 knots. We accelerated violently as the wind hit the sails. It rose higher and the water surface became a mass of whipped-up foam. *Fathom* heeled hard and the lee rail dipped throwing great scoops of water back along the deck. We were starting to sail the hard way – brute strength. For maybe 15 minutes I helmed standing half in the cockpit and half on the weather rail gauging the distance to go before reaching a gap that had appeared and was widening between this brute and the next. The wind rose to over 30 knots and *Fathom* started to vibrate under my feet. I knew by then we were seriously over-canvassed but with no realistic chance of reducing sail I tried to ignore how much more pressure the rig would take. *Fathom* had never heeled as hard as she was then and she was becoming harder to control. Desperately praying that nothing came adrift I gauged I could make the gap so long as I held course and speed. Gripping the wheel and shouting at *Fathom* and myself we punched through an increasingly angry sea. Through the spray I suddenly sensed we were gaining ground towards the small shaft of daylight between both monsters. The next few minutes seemed to last a lifetime but, finally, with huge relief we powered into the gap as if making a home run. Almost immediately the sky began to lighten and 10 minutes later we sailed into sunlight.

Over the next two hours the wind dropped almost completely as the distance between us and the receding masses widened. As the wind disappeared so my levels of acute apprehension did likewise and I reflected that, for the second time on the trip, I had felt a strange sense of danger. Some months later I read Chay Blyth's account of his making the first ever non-stop east-west circumnavigation in 1970 and in which, when at roughly the same position, he wrote:

Still being pushed towards the African coast. Had more squalls last night with one which could only be described as King Squall. I went outside into the cockpit and surrounding me was a great blanket of black cloud. At this stage the wind was about 15 knots . . . and then wham! 40 knots of wind and rain screamed across us.........I shall be delighted to get away from these squalls.........who's a coward? So I'm a coward.

I knew exactly how he felt. He was a very tough ex-paratrooper in a 60ft steel yacht, who had already rowed across the Atlantic with John Ridgeway in 1966. I was pleased to realise that I was not just being a wimp.

During the afternoon the wind remained frustratingly elusive. Given nothing better to do I went below to make a mug of tea and update the log. It was then that I noticed the chartplotter had lost its fix and was no longer telling me my position. Somehow it just didn't seem to be my day. I felt no undue concern and put the reason down to the unusual atmospheric conditions of the last 12 hours. I released my backup hand-held Garmin GPS from the oven, found some fresh batteries and shortly thereafter had a fix. It did not give me any pretty pictures like the chartplotter but an accurate latitude/longitude and my paper Admiralty charts were all I needed to get to Barbados. Having said that, I hoped the chartplotter would sort itself out soon as I rather liked its reassuringly confident screen showing a picture of my position and heading.

Clutching the Garmin I climbed back into the cockpit. I settled into my usual seat in the corner looking aft and watched the receding cloud masses, reflecting how relieved I was to have escaped the threatening conditions of the morning. I was also thankfully surprised not to feel more concerned over the loss of my principal navigation system. However, I was becalmed again. Hearing the genoa flap, I turned to look forward and froze. Sliding over the horizon in front of me was the top of another huge mass of black darkness.

I vividly remember my feelings right then – physically tired and mentally exhausted. I knew it had been one thing to try and cope during daylight with what had seemed such menacing conditions but, with darkness falling, I felt wholly ill-equipped to face the same potential threat all over again in the dark. Whilst I had managed so far to avoid all but the very edge of these ITCZ brutes I was more than worried that the 41 knots I had experienced would translate into something very much more substantial towards their centre. I sat in the cockpit for a while trying to work out my best plan of action, but I knew that in the dark trying to surf across the face of these monstrous squalls was a non-starter. The tension and concentration since dawn had also taken its toll on my energy levels. Becalmed as I was, there seemed no way I could get myself out of the way as this new approaching cloud mass spread not only across but also above the horizon. With little energy left, I realised that the most sensible option was to take down all sail and just sit out anything that came my way. Clipping on, I slowly furled and bagged both genoa and main before slumping sweatily below decks and calling Shaunagh on the satellite phone. I wanted to talk my situation through with her. This was the first time that I consciously decided to tell Shaunagh I was concerned and realised it would be asking a lot of her to talk things through when there was nothing she could do to help. She was astonishing. Quietly and remarkably calmly we noted my position and went through the emergency 'grab' bag that I kept at the foot of the companionway– flares, water, radio, emergency beacon, laser torches, GPS, torch, some food tins, a tin opener and a small basic fishing kit. Staying on the line I then secured the grab bag in the cockpit before checking that the emergency liferaft, fixed to the transom, was ready to be released. There was nothing more we could do. Promising her I would call at the first sign of anything going wrong and, if it didn't, certainly at first light, we quietly hung up. I realised with a real pang just how much she meant to me. I also knew how completely alone we both felt at that moment.

Looking back calmly now, I can see this was the moment when I reached my lowest mental point. It resulted from 12 days mental and physical pressure dealing with Delta, broken ribs, being followed at night, a second threatened storm, growing concern over the batteries, the loss of my principal navigational system and the unexpected instability of the weather cumulating in these menacing ITCZ horrors. In the big scheme of things none was overly dramatic but combined with my level of tiredness I let it get to me mentally. I can genuinely say that for the first time in my life I felt drained, not just physically as had happened many times in close rowing races but mentally as well. Bluntly, I felt knackered.

It was interesting that I felt as I did on seeing this next mass of cloud slide over the horizon. I am not by nature someone given to feeling sorry for myself. I am also stubborn and dislike any form of mental 'giving-up' no matter how trivial. For a moment, though, I wobbled badly as both my common sense and logic were briefly displaced by some pretty woolly thinking. Why on earth I thought an emergency inflatable liferaft would be called for or terribly useful when I was on a modern 41ft GRP boat is beyond me. If the boat went down, the liferaft would not be far behind it. I realise now that, tired beyond normal levels, my mind became quite distracted by weird ideas. The interesting thing was that once I had spoken with Shaunagh, worked out a plan of action and organised myself for seemingly any eventuality I started to function much better. I think this happened simply through completing the physical and mental activity of checking and preparing the grab bag. This allowed me to focus my mind on something constructive and not the weather. For 10 minutes I forgot my brain was telling me I was tired. Disengaging from the oppressive pressure that had increasingly built up over last 12 hours and engaging it in a relatively mundane task seemed to break the spell and made me feel back in control. It also made me forget I had been frightened.

Feeling better and more organised I accepted this could be a long night. In the eerie silence of a boat drifting in an ocean with no sails up I set about making something to eat even though I had lost all appetite. After forcing something down, I then lay down to try and grab some sleep.

Amazingly, I did and for very nearly two hours. By the time I woke up, it was dark outside.

10 Dec – 09:17 GPS – pos: N17°18' | W036°23'

Distance covered in previous 24 hours	59 nm
CL total	1,531 nm
HL total	1,572 nm
+/–	–41 nm

When I first woke, around midnight, there was little noise or movement. I lay on my berth for a few moments listening to *Fathom*. My head was hard up against the hull and I could sense the ocean on the other side silently sliding past. Warily, I got up, pulled on some clothes and stood at the bottom of the companionway. It was strangely quiet. I climbed the steps and went on deck peering into the surrounding darkness. Anxiously looking around the boat I expected to find myself surrounded by what I had seen approaching at sunset. Instead, though cloudy, I looked up and could see broken clouds and glimpses of stars. Of the massive sinister squalls there was no trace. I could hardly believe it. The change since I had gone below was as if I had gone to sleep in one world and awoken in another. I cannot tell you how relieved I felt. It was as if a huge weight as massive as the blackness of the clouds themselves had lifted. I slumped down in the cockpit and, forgetting my lack of sleep, put my head back and deeply inhaled the peace of the night and the quiet stillness of the ocean. After the raw tension and tiredness of the previous 20 hours I felt as if I had won a reprieve and been released from some bad nightmare. It was wonderfully calming and I suddenly felt the warm and humid silence of the night surround me like a comforting arm around my shoulders.

For a long time I just sat in the cockpit unaware of time. With no wind to worry about nothing seemed to matter and my mind started to ramble through a maze of strange thoughts as it always does when I'm really tired. I wondered whether my father had ever been through this type of weather on his trans-Atlantic or trans-Pacific. He had certainly never mentioned anything either verbally or in his logs and now I would be unable to ask him. That seemed a pity. If he had, I would have been interested to have compared our reactions. I didn't think mine had been very composed albeit *Fathom* and I had got through in one piece. I realised that the old adage of 'a problem shared is a problem halved' certainly would have applied over the last 20 hours – probably the only time in the entire trip that I recall thinking that having someone else on board could possibly have been welcomed. I also wondered if I really had managed to escape from the blackened mass of the squalls. They had seemed so big and outside of them there had been so little wind that I could hardly believe I was far from their vast threatening shadows. I couldn't see much in the darkness but somehow I sensed the danger was passed. The night seemed at peace and it felt very calming. After a while, I slowly became more aware of my surroundings and, looking at my watch, I saw it was 02.30hrs. Through the humid darkness I sensed a very faint breeze whispering across the water from the SE. After so patiently enduring the calms between squalls, I sorted myself out, climbed into my harness and thankfully hoisted all sail. At 04.30hrs the breeze coughed and then died. Reluctantly, I went through the reverse process and lowered all sail.

For the next four hours we sat quietly lolling around again in a very slight swell.

With nothing better to do and still not feeling like a return to my berth, I went forward in the pitch dark to undo the chain I had placed around the shroud as an earth. It was then that I got an enormous shock – not electrical but physical. As I was crawling along the narrow side deck, something big suddenly moved immediately alongside in the inky black water and took a deep rumbling breath. I was not alone. Scrambling backwards on all fours dragging my lifeline as fast as I could into the sanctuary of the cockpit I turned my head torch on and nervously scanned the water's surface. Flying fish on my deck were one thing but this sounded on an altogether different scale. Although I couldn't see anything I definitely felt a presence close by and quickly slid below to turn the stereo on quietly to give some indication where I was to whatever was in the water alongside. As fate would have it I had a blues CD loaded already that I had been given by my son's beautiful girl-friend and which I liked hugely. Sadly, my visitor clearly had a different taste in music as, when I came back on deck, it seemed to have gone. For a while I stood quietly straining eyes and ears but it never returned. I have no idea what it was.

Somewhat disappointed, I went below again to make myself some coffee before returning to my normal position in the cockpit to wait for some wind. At 08.30hrs just enough puff from the SE appeared again so, guess what, all the sails went back up and I sedately headed off at 2 knots albeit in the wrong direction. I didn't care. I had wind, I was moving and I could clear the ITCZ.

Despite my very disturbed night, the abject tiredness of the previous evening had started to evaporate as soon as I found I was not in the middle of something nasty. As dawn broke I was still in the cockpit and sat with real pleasure watching the colours emerge, merge and then be washed away as the sun broke over the surface of the horizon and a new day started. I went below and re-appeared five minutes later with my healthy alternative to the bacon sarnie – Greek yoghurt mixed with pumpkin and sunflower seeds, honey and all washed down by a large mug of sweet tea. As the sun rose what breeze had come with dawn disappeared and *Fathom* and I were left on a smooth and gently undulating ocean swell glassy in appearance. The sails slatted slowly back and forth as the swell effortlessly lifted us up and down whilst whispering zephyrs swung from all compass points throughout the morning.

Around midday small wind ripples started skating across the water surface and then, gradually, began to fill more consistently from the east. Slowly I brought the helm round onto a more useful heading and towards a distant line of white and puffy squall clouds on the horizon. Two hours later, we sailed slowly and sedately under the line and were joined by a pod of dolphins with a young Torville and Dean double act – somersaults, double axels, triple salcos and resounding belly flops – they had quite a repertoire and all at up to 15ft in the air. Wonderful entertainment, beautiful to watch and immensely restoring for my spirits. I felt I was being escorted away from the bad weather.

That day was in stark contrast to the previous 36 hours and I spent most of it happy to coast along not pushing for full speed. Time is a luxury that we all take for granted and rarely relish. Back in the office I would spend my time having one meeting after another, talking with clients, writing reports that should probably have been finished earlier, juggling telephone calls and impatiently rushing through the day. I would then struggle home on the underground, quickly showering and changing before heading off for drinks and dinner, probably in two different places. Even on holiday I am rubbish at relaxing and spend my life in the garden, by a river, up a mountain, on a boat or generally twitching. In total contrast, that morning I just sat in the cockpit and enjoyed the space, quiet and spiritual peace of being alone on an ocean. It made me think of the old Arab proverb that no man's soul should travel faster than the speed of a galloping camel. My camel was doing a slow three knots and it felt good.

Over a lunch of tinned white asparagus, cold ham, dry-toasted granary rolls and mayonnaise I realised that I was past the geographical half-way stage. That reminded me that, tucked away in the saloon, was a package my son, Drummond, had given me with the strict instruction to open it only when I reached this point. Going below I re-emerged into the cockpit with a can of beer in one hand

and a large padded envelope in the other. It was something of a mini treasure trove. It contained a miscellanea of a pre-recorded DVD by him, a woolly hat, three home made cards, toe clippers, tweezers, and a couple of other assorted personal grooming items clearly considered vital by university students. Excited by the DVD and the thought of seeing him, I took the disc below, extracted my computer from its' Pelican shock-proof case and set it up on the saloon table keen to see what he had recorded and to be reminded of his smile and voice. Sadly, the laptop had been playing up ever since I had left Las Palmas and whilst the DVD played, it was at a speed that was so slow it made him look like a village idiot and sound like a Martian. I tried several times to make it work properly but, with huge regret, I finally turned it off and put the computer back in its case. As I did so, I had quite a pang at not being able to hear his voice and what he was saying to me. I would have to wait for the real thing once back in London. Stowing the Pelican case behind me in a locker I sat somewhat gloomily at the saloon table and for a while my mind mulled over my relationship with him and how very different it was to the one I had with my father.

Never having experienced a normal father/son relationship or even an emotional bond with my father I had relied on trial and error (plenty of both) in developing relationships with my children and step-children. My mother has been a rock throughout my life which has gone a long way to limiting a number of the 'errors'. I owe her a very great deal. However, there are some gender limits as to how far any heterosexual son can look to his mother as a suitable role model and not having a corresponding male role model had its moments. My first couple of made-to-measure suits on leaving Oxford were fine examples of 1970s High Street chic with flared trouser bottoms rather than City-gentlemen's bespoke suits; the floral cravat that I wore for my first wedding has been a source of personal embarrassment ever since and turning down my very first job offer in 1977 from Cazenove can hardly be described as 'informed'. However, my favourite is the two hours I spent, aged 15, in a barn at a dance lying next to one of the most beautiful girls in West Sussex in a petrified trance of complete emotional and physical confusion. I think I even pretended to fall asleep. Happily, none of our children have ever needed any advice in that direction. Drum and I have also spent many happy moments in conversation about twin vents, square pockets and the correct length for suit jackets.

I have always loved my children. There have been times when I have found that emotion difficult to display naturally and openly. In my own role as a father, how much of that is due to not seeing my own father for much more than a couple of weeks a year as I grew up is hard to tell. It seems an easy excuse. He wasn't exactly the ideal example anyway. My own divorce can't have helped either. Certainly it meant I didn't find fulfilling the role of a father straightforward and in too many ways I am still bad at involving them in the things I do. As a young boy and teenager I recall increasingly making my own life and amusements in the absence of a central male figure to watch and copy. Even when we stayed with him, my father was rarely around and when he was he still expected us to amuse ourselves whilst he dug in his automatic watering, pruned trees and shrubs or read technical reference books on hybrid cross-pollination. It was my stepmother who made the effort when we stayed with them in the same way our children will recognise Shaunagh's efforts today. I know I am better than my father but that hardly warrants any medals. At least with my children – Soph, Drum and Rosie – it has been more of a joint effort. Like most families, we have all worked for strong relationships and probably each of us has had difficulty at times finding the right vocabulary. But at least we have all been looking and trying. I count myself enormously fortunate and grateful to them and my step-children, Elizabeth and Harry, for being so patient with me as I have grappled with the concept and responsibilities of fatherhood. They have all done much of the teaching.

I say this as relationships are not given but earned, especially the worthwhile ones. The only people who most of us are automatically pre-programmed to love unconditionally are our parents. However, at some time in each of our lives, whether aged 12, 25 or 50, most of us will examine whether that unconditional love is deserved. We do that with our parents in the same way that our children will do so with us. The answer may not always be positive and, if that is the conclusion reached, I believe it takes a while to accept that this is not unnatural. In my case, I had long since worked out that whilst my mother had given so much and was so deserving in that emotional examination my father had not. Having reached that conclusion, the question I think I found myself searching for was, would he have cared?

I found that a difficult question to address. Not difficult because I didn't know the answer – I did, he didn't care – but because in some way emotionally for me it diminished him in my eyes. We may not have been close but I admired a number of his achievements. However, just as there is a fundamental difference between being alone and being lonely, so too is there a difference between admiring someone's achievements and admiring the individual who undertook them. Both sentiments can be exclusive of one another. But much as I would like to have been proud of my father for some of what he did he made it too difficult. His total lack of interest in others alienated any such feelings for me. As it is, I find it difficult to understand even how much I liked him.

He did, however, help spark my early interest in boats and sailing. I am grateful to him for that – but gratitude is an entirely different and less valuable emotion.

11 Dec – 09:51 GPS – pos: N16°50′ | W038°11′

Distance covered in previous 24 hours	95 nm
CL total	1,626 nm
HL total	1,692 nm
+/–	–66 nm

First thing this morning I thought I had found northeast winds at last. After 14 days at sea on what has always been called the trade wind route they had been frustratingly absent. They had been replaced by winds from every other direction but with no consistency. However, this morning I could see clouds clearly suggesting the near proximity of trade winds but, even so, the best I was being offered was weak northerlies of around eight knots. I had achieved a rather pedestrian 96 miles for the last 24 hours in return for quite an amount of hard physical labour and I was getting increasingly fed up again with not making better 24 hour runs.

On top of that, last night when I started the generator to charge the batteries it had sounded like an old farm tractor in thick mud. Going rapidly on deck I had peered over the side of the boat to see if water was coming out of the cooling exhaust as normal but saw only smoke. Bugger! Racing below, I promptly turned the generator off before it overheated. I guessed it was either a blocked water intake or a problem with the impeller on the water pump. Raising and securing the companionway steps, I stuck my head and hands into the engine compartment and checked the water intake. It was clear. As it was getting dark and the generator was in a sound-proof housing at the bottom of the vast cockpit locker under mountains of spare sails and 36 cans of beer, I decided to leave a fiddly investigation of the impeller until the morning. Meanwhile, I turned the main engine on to charge and was pleasantly surprised at how quickly it did the job. However, I did wonder what using the main engine would do to my dwindling diesel supplies. Pushing that worry aside, I contemplated the joys of getting into the cavernous cockpit locker and accessing the generator to check and change impellers – not the easiest of jobs, especially in a rolling sea. I also had an unsettling image of emptying the locker of sails and climbing into it only for the locker lid to slam shut over me leaving Otto and *Fathom* to sail serenely on with me incarcerated with the beer. I suppose I would have been quite happy for a while.

This morning, given the cloud formations, I was more hopeful that the winds would begin to fill in and the push for Barbados could start in earnest as I got close to the last 1,000 miles. It didn't feel as if I had been on my own for two weeks although I had been surprised when coming on deck before dawn to see, way above me, the faint flashing of an aircraft's lights – I could just make out the tiny silhouette of its wings and fuselage far above me against the night sky. I was surprised because of my un-expected but immediate emotional reaction at knowing other human beings were in that plane; I was not completely alone. However, I realised how much smaller I must be, not even a dot on the ocean. I stared up at it for a long time imagining what the sleepy passengers and crew were doing and wondered if any were looking down towards me and my part of the ocean. I found that thought strangely reassuring. I also found it strangely intrusive and unsettling. In the last nine days I had only briefly seen one other boat and three men. Other than that I had seen no other signs of human life – no flotsam in the water, no vapour trails in the sky, nothing man-made apart from *Fathom* and me. Much to my astonishment, throughout it all I had not had one moment when I had felt lonely. I was happy with myself and truly enjoying the solitude and surroundings. Moitessier expressed similar feelings when he wrote, 'I was slowly beginning to realise what a huge treasure solitude had brought me. At last, I had time to be alone with myself, time to contemplate what was around me. Before, everything had been a blur. During all those years I had never stopped running. And now a great calm had been spreading within me, a calm I could savour'.

After the trip, when I spoke with Shaunagh about this lack of any feeling of loneliness she said, with typical bluntness, that it was remarkable what my lack of imagination had allowed me to do. I rather suspect she was right albeit I was genuinely surprised to learn at first hand of the difference between loneliness and solitude. As a young student I had lived in Paris for four months surrounded by millions of others living and walking within inches of me every day and, for a variety of reasons (mostly immature) had never felt lonelier. Here was I, now, mid-Atlantic with not a soul for possibly hundreds of miles and I had rarely felt so completely at home and fulfilled. Very odd. I suppose that whilst not noticeably feeling affected by any loneliness in those first fourteen days, if I tried I could think of a couple of times when I would have willingly shared some of the sights and experiences. However, for the rest I would, unquestionably, have been deeply protective of my undisturbed freedom.

I was right in thinking that the winds would fill in on sighting trade wind clouds. Once watery dawn had done her thing and given way to her sister, broad daylight, things started to change. As the morning wore on the sea got steadily bigger as the barometer started falling until, over the horizon, marched massed squall clouds. They seemed less threatening than those of two days ago but in front of them was piled up an unusually broken and disturbed sea to around 20 ft. For most of the afternoon I ran parallel to the squall line as it was big and moving fast. In the early evening I saw what looked like even worse weather coming up behind it. Two hours before sunset I decided to change tack and head across its path to try and clear the other side before the onset of darkness. I went to triple reef all round.

Knowing that I would require all my concentration for the next couple of hours I put my regular evening call through to Shaunagh even though it was earlier than normal. It was nice and reassuring to hear her voice and we had a quick chat as I explained how I was getting on. I tried to make it sound all very normal but was increasingly aware from the sea state and cloud mass that conditions were deteriorating. We blew one another kisses and I quickly turned the Iridium off and stowed it safely. From then on the concentration started – I never felt overpowered but did feel myself becoming increasingly tense as the movement of the boat became more violent as the wind speed and sea state picked up. Twice I misjudged the unexpected steepness of the waves and fell badly and heavily off the side of large breakers thinking we would broach. I found it hard to understand how the conditions could deteriorate so quickly. It was a sharp reminder of the dangers of being alone but I could do little immediately to slow the boat down. It was hairy sailing and not a little scary in the fast fading daylight.

For two hours I held my course luffing up in the strongest gusts (30–35 knots) to avoid being over pressed. Sometime just after sunset, and with very considerable relief, I cleared the far side of the squall line and was met by the sight of a rising full moon and a wonderfully clear night sky. After the previous two hours it was extraordinary how suddenly it went from bad to near normal conditions, almost as if opening a door into a different world. I had expected the wind to drop substantially but, to my grateful surprise, it steadied at a full force 5 and, under reefed headsail and main, we pushed on fast into the night.

Putting Otto on, I somewhat wearily went below to have a hot shower and cook myself another Thai curry. Towelling myself dry and then preparing the necessary ingredients I realised that I had started to rather enjoy thinking about what I wanted to eat. Although loving all types of food, I have never been a good cook and so have spent very little time thinking about food other than when looking at a menu. On the trip I did, however, surprise myself by finding myself on many days wondering what I would like to eat. Often such thoughts foundered on my subsequent inability to locate the chosen item(s) amongst the mass of tins, cartons, jars and boxes crammed into each locker. Even aided by the meticulous list made by Max, my brother-in-law, of what went into each locker when we first stowed the boat it proved, on some occasions, finger breakingly impossible. The most frustrating discovery was when I found the drawer containing all the rice, pasta, dried beans and couscous jammed shut. That removed a whole section from my potential menu as after inspection, it appeared that I would have to dismantle half the cabin to gain access. Accordingly, some days for lunch I had been bone idle and just grabbed the first thing that came to hand. This had produced some interesting culinary combinations – anchovies with peaches, oatcakes with white asparagus and marmite, the unforgettable fruitcake with mayonnaise and salami. However, for supper I tended to try and make something a little less avant-garde.

Pre-packed ready-made cooking sauces allow someone with my culinary skills to feel like Rick Stein. With my iPod on in the background and a glass of wine to hand I hummed away quietly to myself in the galley preparing the food – diced onions, chopped chicken, lamb, beef or fresh fish. This was then topped up with a few tins of mushrooms, beans, carrots, potatoes or pulses. Finally, I sliced the top off one of the sauce envelopes, squirted it over the contents and, hey presto, a gourmet dinner for one. On some occasions I was so pleased with the result I actually took some video clips of the bubbling ensemble. I felt I had scaled a gastronomic peak.

On this particular evening the curry made me feel instantly re-invigorated. It seemed to lift my spirits as well as the roof of my mouth and, once I had tidied up, I went back on deck and sat for a long while in the corner of the cockpit under the spray-hood looking aft.

The sheer beauty of the scene was awesome. In the moonlight, *Fathom* was snaking across the surface leaving a foaming wake behind her in an almost straight line like a vapour trail in the sky. The mixture of speed and wave would cause her to heel and twist into each wave rhythmically. Every now and again she would sharply accelerate across a patch of flatter water. It was a magical hour or so, mesmerising in its movement and power. For a long while I sat in the corner of the moonlit cockpit completely lost under the spell cast by the beauty of it all. Sometime around midnight, though feeling exhilarated by my surroundings, I realised that I needed to try and grab a couple of hours sleep. Reluctantly sliding down the companionway and undressing, I lay on my berth but with my mind refusing to succumb completely to tiredness. I drifted in and out of shallow sleep as I listened to the ocean hissing past my head only inches away on the other side of the hull. Several times I got up and just stood on the bottom step of the companionway looking out at the rolling surface of the ocean cut by our single foaming trail under a full moon. I have never before felt or seen such effortless power or sensed such harmony in natural forces. I felt very humbled. I also felt deeply privileged to be there, just *Fathom* and me. I wish we could have had more days and nights like that.

12 Dec – 07:21 GPS – pos: N16°24' | W040°18'

Distance covered in previous 24 hours	141 nm
CL total	1,767 nm
HL total	1,812 nm
+/–	–45 nm

Given the fast conditions yesterday and overnight, we clocked up a 24 hour run of something around 140 miles.

It was a relief to show what could be done with the right conditions. In retrospect it turned out that the weather in November and December 2005 for most transatlantic aspirants was the most awkward for many years. Storms, light winds and the absence of firmly established trade winds made for unusually lengthy crossings and the informal 20 day target I had quietly set myself was clearly not going to happen. During all the planning I had been back through the records for ARC entrants over the previous 5 years and seen that similar boats to *Fathom* had taken anywhere between 17 and 25 days. I realised this was for crewed boats as the ARC does not accept solo entrants but, nonetheless, hoped I could split the two if I was lucky. I had even briefly wondered whether I could beat Shaunagh to Barbados and greet her on her arrival rather than vice versa.

Sadly, no such luck. This morning we were back to funereal pace as the weather had clearly blown itself out over the last 24 hours and we were rapidly slipping back again on the daily runs I needed even to equal my father's 23 days. It was a nice dawn though.

With light winds yet again, albeit with quite a large swell, I decided I would at least see if I could fix the non-functioning chartplotter now that the main engine was so much more effective charging the batteries. I sat and read the entire manual, tried a number of reset options before resorting to the default setting. One push of that button and the chartplotter burst into technicolour life with a series of beeps and there, in the middle of the screen, was the boat's image and with all instrument readings showing correctly. I felt somewhere between Einstein and the village idiot. It had obviously not been a problem caused by atmospheric conditions but by my electrical problems and lack of power.

Not wanting a repeat electrical problem as I started the final 1,000 miles I decided to continue using the main engine for charging and not fix the generator impeller. It now strikes me that a generator is useful on a boat if needing to iron a skirt, blow-dry your hair or microwave a soufflé – other than that almost entirely useless. An expensive lesson.

The other lesson I had been learning was the downside to *Fathom's* internal layout. Ever since Delta I had realised that the forward heads were impractical to use as, whilst stern facing and on the middle line of the boat, in any seaway my bottom and loo seat were in less physical contact than my head and the roof. The results were always unpredictable and always slightly unsatisfactory. As a consequence I used the amidships heads. These were positioned to port of the saloon and quite confined in space for someone my height. Whilst ideal for Mediterranean cruising, they did pose a considerable uphill challenge for me to enter in the wilder conditions of the Atlantic when on port tack. This led to the interesting question and inevitable physical struggle of when to lower trousers – after going in or before? To lower them after entering required the skills and agility of a very small Russian gymnast. To lower them before was even more challenging as I was reduced to making small but increasingly desperate hops and skips like an Emperor penguin just to get over the lip of the door into the heads. Even once safely in, there was the additional problem of staying on the seat as the angle at which I then sat meant the door had to be used for support. Bursting back into the saloon in the seated position, hands flailing for support and legs ensnared in lowered trousers, was a real and unedifying prospect. To make matters worse, the seat was too small. I experimented in a number of positions but, whatever I did, the seat only accommodated one buttock and both balls or both buttocks and one ball. It proved impossible (and eye watering) to fit both buttocks and both balls.

A personal sense of the ridiculous helps when sailing.

13 Dec – 08:02 GPS – pos: N16°01' | W042°42'

Distance covered in previous 24 hours	142 nm
CL total	1,909 nm
HL total	1,932 nm
+/–	–23 nm

Today, just after dawn, we crossed the 1,000 mile marker to Barbados. Coincidentally, that also put me exactly midway between my two closest points of land, Barbados and the Cape Verde Islands, 997 miles in either direction. This was the point at which I was furthest from land (other than the sea bed 3.5 miles under my keel) and, briefly, I felt quite exposed at that thought. I had no reason to feel so but realised that on a practical note if anything went wrong now it was unrealistic to hope for any swift help. It reminded me of Blondie Hassler's famous comment that those going long distance in boats *should be prepared to die like gentlemen* rather than rely on others to risk their lives to assist. My upper lip never trembled but I was still only a dot in the vast expanse of the ocean, probably several hundreds of miles off any shipping route and now entering what I called the empty quarter of the trip. I had no idea as to how close I was to another vessel and assumed it could easily be another couple of hundred miles. I imagined myself standing alone at Marble Arch in London with the nearest person standing on the Arc de Triomphe in Paris. Quite some thought.

On a more practical note, I had managed to reel off another 140 miles in the last 24 hours. That was a good result given that I was at last firmly in the trade winds and always reduced sail to reefed main only at night to save panic attacks if one of the customary trade wind squalls came along. I was also running mainly dead downwind so the genoa was blanketed by the mainsail and did not draw properly – much of the time it hung about and flapped like a flightless dodo. At night I now almost always furled it fully to avoid being woken by the noise.

Unexpectedly, I was finding my substantially reduced and broken sleep of the last 15 days less debilitating than I would have expected. I had long stopped worrying about waking frequently and not getting 'enough' sleep. Quite often I just lay in the dark on my berth listening to the various noises that *Fathom* was making or thinking of something interesting, but brief, for the morning blog. It seemed a very natural rhythm to have adjusted to. The physical training of the last year was also clearly paying off as, in the early planning stages for the trip, I had realised that to cope with expected short sleep periods I would need to achieve a high level of fitness, higher than I had enjoyed for many years. It had not always been easy or enjoyable. However, I was becoming very grateful for the effort. In the nine months of training before I started, I remember often wanting to stop halfway through a set of 4 x 100 sit-ups or 5 kilometres into an 8 kilometre run. There were days when my legs or arms just felt leaden and unwilling to respond to continual exercise. That was when the Oxford Boat Race training mentality re-appeared and took over to make me finish each exercise properly. It was a good feeling to rediscover that mental focus.

Whilst generally feeling better than I had expected, the slightest lapse in concentration meant mistakes were still all too easy to make. Yesterday the wind gods favoured me with some fast but roughish sailing. An hour before dusk I needed to go forward to take down the main and so donned my safety harness, picked up the loose end of the safety line and clipped it to the harness. Cautiously crawling forward and then standing on the coach roof in a 12ft swell to bag the main I realised the boat was going to roll heavily. Changing my grip to hold on to the boom, it swung me backwards such that my feet stayed on the coach roof but my bum and shoulders were over the guard rails and the sea. Twice it happened and each time I clearly remember being very grateful that I was clipped on, as one slip of my grip would have had me over the side. When I had finished, I dropped to my knees and crawled back into the cockpit. It was only then that, with complete horror, I saw that I had never been clipped on at all. In my tiredness I hadn't realised that my harness had already been attached to the safety line when I had first put it on. The loose end I had picked up I should have clipped to the jackstay on the deck. Instead I had clipped it to my harness. I had attached both ends of the safety line to me and none to the boat. I was truly furious with myself, well past the 'silly sod' stage, and had the extraordinary experience of becoming momentarily two people, skipper and crew. As skipper I threw myself down in a corner of the cockpit and really shouted at myself for my utter stupidity. As crew I was made to feel completely and utterly irresponsible. As skipper and crew we had both frightened one another and I learned deeply from that experience. Tiredness can be a quick killer.

My father felt likewise crossing the Atlantic and put it well when writing:

I am sure the greatest danger at sea is that of falling overboard. If you trip up and fall into the water when underway, one is dead. Really the only practical method of avoiding this peril is to take extreme care. I used to think that if the boat had been floating like an airship 10,000 feet up, one would have been on hands and knees every time one moved up the side-decks.

He was right and I had given myself a bad shock.

14 Dec – 07:53 GPS – pos: N15°41' | W044°50'

Distance covered in previous 24 hours	125 nm
CL total	2,034 nm
HL total	2,052 nm
+/–	–18 nm

Well, what a contrast. Yesterday was fantastic sailing with the chute up for 9 hours ripping large chunks out of the remaining mileage. Last night, in sharp contrast, was pretty grim as the wind dropped to around seven knots and swung throughout the night. Yet again I had another night long on gybing, rolling and rattling but short on sleep. The one discovery I did make at 04.22hrs and which frankly, at that stage, ranked right up there with the electric light-bulb and the microchip was a dirty, single, simple wax earplug! Disgusting but wonderful.

After a short but wonderfully deep one-sided earplug-induced sleep, I finally woke an hour before dawn and poked my head into the cockpit – clear skies. The wind was still light but hoping it would back into the northerly quarter at some stage, I rigged and raised the chute after another dawn breakfast in the cockpit.

I had now been 17 days without sight of land and today, during the course of the morning, I began to experience the most curious sense – that of sailing uphill. It was the weirdest feeling and made complete nonsense of any known law of physics. However, there was no doubting that for most of the day I was travelling across and slightly up the side of a gently sloping hill. I spent some time trying to ignore this unusual development but each time I looked around the boat sure enough there was the top of the hill just in front and to the right of me whilst the sea fell away downhill on the other side of the boat to port. I have no idea if it was something to do with the angle of light, the sea state or 17 days of unbroken nothingness on the horizon but it was a very strong sensation and was to stay with me intermittently for most of the rest of the trip. I am sure part of it was being heeled to starboard continually in south east and easterly winds. When my father was solo in the Pacific he also experienced a mild form of nuttiness albeit manifested differently to mine. He wrote;

In this world of only two external elements, a floor of water and a roof of sky, another doubt began to assail me – that the boat was really stationary, stuck motionless between the two hemispheres and that all the fuss of one's 40ft world, the rolling and bouncing and splashing and even the moving, was just a phenomenon suspended for ever at the centre of the featureless line of the horizon.

In my case I also suspect it was something to do with the fact I had also been running parallel for the last couple of days to the ITCZ that had re-appeared along the horizon some 10 miles to port. I felt as if it was trying to suck me back into its maw and psychologically I was pushing uphill to get away. When discussing this re-appearance of the ITCZ in one of my last satellite phone calls with AWC, Simon Keeling had asked me to take some photographs. In all the years they had been providing weather information to transatlantic yachtsmen he said few sailors they had spoken with had run parallel and in sight of the ITCZ for as long as I had.

It was also the day that, uphill of me, I noticed a very small smudge on the horizon. By the time I saw it, the chute was already up and the sea state was making us roll too much to focus my binoculars properly to see any details clearly. However, after a couple of hours I could make out the tip of a mast ahead and that I was inexorably sailing faster and gaining ground. As with the French yacht six days earlier, I tried calling them up on VHF, this time in English, French, German and Spanish. Had I received a reply in anything other than English I would have had been seriously challenged but, as it was, the radio remained mute. I found this surprising and began to wonder what would happen if I had needed to put out a mayday. On my experience to date I had seen only two yachts in fourteen days and clearly neither of them had their radio on. Before leaving, I was aware that without an SSB radio for transmitting longer distances I was disadvantaged. Hence having two emergency satellite beacons (EPIRBs) on board. Bluntly, it appeared I could have blown myself up, sunk or caught fire within VHF range of another boat and never been rescued, far less noticed. I'm not even sure a liferaft would have been any use either in the event of having to abandon ship. If other sailing boats did not respond to radio calls from boats within sight (if I could see them they must have been able to see me), what chance of being seen in something the size of a small dinghy? That was one of the reasons that another of the better pieces of safety equipment I had on board were two laser torches. They had a range of over 10 miles and, at which distance, the beam is five miles wide. I had bought them in America on one of my last business trips to New York. On the return sail from Barbados to Spain, the crew hove to in bad weather some three miles from a large tanker and, by radio, requested a test of the lasers. The response from the bridge of the tanker was instantaneous and quite nautical in flavour owing to the strength of the beam. Such torches are powerful but completely safe and I have always taken the view that it is better to be seen than lost.

Although I didn't know it at the time, a very real rescue had taken place of an ARC entrant not far from where I was. Their lifeline was being part of the rally where regular daily radio contact is strictly maintained throughout the entire fleet. *Caliso*, a 42ft Swedish Yacht owned by friends, had departed Las Palmas on November 17th exactly a week before me as a member of the ARC fleet. They had pushed slowly south in light winds to avoid Delta and had made slow progress down towards the Cape Verde Islands before swinging westwards towards their ultimate destination of Antigua. After some 10 days they noticed water coming in around the keel box. After a close examination and a subsequent crew meeting, it was decided to put out an immediate call for assistance. Being part of the ARC their radio call was quickly picked up by other entrants and relayed to the rally organisers in the UK. That night the crew slept on deck as there was real concern that *Caliso's* keel could detach and she would capsize. Anyone inside would have been trapped. Two other ARC entrants arrived and stood-to until the arrival of a bulk carrier, *MV Endless*, the next morning who had steamed overnight and then winched all the crew members off. *Caliso* was abandoned.

The story did have a happy ending. *Caliso* was recovered two weeks later having drifted into mid-Atlantic. She was towed back to the Cape Verde islands and, from there, shipped back to the Mediterranean for full repairs. All costs were covered by the insurance company.

Happily, I knew nothing of these events and did not run into *Caliso* drifting aimlessly and empty like the *Marie Celeste*. Had I done so I would have been hugely alarmed knowing that Fleur and five other crew should have been on board.

15 Dec – 07:43 GPS – pos: N15°22′ | W046°53′

Distance covered in previous 24 hours	*128 nm*
CL total	*2,162 nm*
HL total	*2,172 nm*
+/–	*–10 nm*

At last, I managed six hours' sleep and felt reborn. I was up on deck three times but did have one two-hour slot undisturbed. Fantastic. The only missing ingredient was a hot, deep bath – I would have been in heaven.

The day before, even with the chute up for another nine hours, was rather pedestrian and totalled 125 miles for the previous 24hrs. However, overnight had seen a change in the weather with cloud and slightly stronger winds. Under full main we maintained a better-than-hoped-for speed around 5.5 knots throughout the night and shortly after dawn I readied the chute for another day's work.

I had been hoping that as I got closer to Barbados the easterly (trade) winds would finally begin to fill in and become more consistent. They seemed to have done so. The one factor that I had not expected was for the seas to increase as well. However, in the last 24 hours I had started to notice the wave height was getting bigger than I had previously experienced for the given wind speed. I was to find this continued to be the case and resulted from the sea-bed rising dramatically from 16,000 feet to 9,000 feet on the approach to the Caribbean islands and heaping the swell up as it shelved. This miscalculation may well have been partly responsible for what happened next.

I had been making reasonable pace throughout the day in 10 – 12 knots of wind but with the sea state making the boat surf involuntarily from time to time on the top of the larger waves. When that happened the boat picked up enough speed to take the wind out of the chute which then collapsed. As the wave passed under the boat we slowed down allowing the wind to fill the chute again. This it did with quite a wrench, a process repeated every minute or so throughout the day. The incessant action shook the whole rig and for much of the time I hand-helmed to avoid the worst of such shocks. I suspect that such continuous stress caused the problem I found when I went forward an hour before sunset – I snuffed the chute easily but found I couldn't lower it. The halyard holding the sausage near the top of the mast was stuck fast and wouldn't budge. Quickly grabbing binoculars I clambered along the side decks and went as far forward as possible. Lying down on my back and focusing the binoculars I could see the halyard emerging from near the masthead and then suddenly saw the sheave (through which it should have run freely) twisted sideways and jammed under it. For twenty minutes, in rapidly fading light, I jostled and tugged the halyard in a desperate attempt to get some movement. It was not a safe option to leave the sausage up the mast. If I couldn't get it down I would have to try and tie it off somehow to stop it swinging around the rigging as much as possible. I had mast steps to the first spreader but was worried that the radar and radar reflector mounted above that would suffer damage if I really couldn't get it down. After what seemed like a lifetime, a small amount of halyard started to pay out and, after more tugging, it finally started to pay out faster. It felt as if the halyard was being dragged over a jagged metallic surface but that was of little immediate concern to me having released the jam. Finally, the whole thing was down, including the offending sheave, in a jumbled mess on deck around my feet.

With huge relief, I coiled the sheets and bagged the sausage, tying the whole package carefully along the side netting on the foredeck. I checked the halyard and found it was badly frayed just below the snap-shackle. On the basis I was unlikely to raise the chute again, I clipped and tightened it to the foot of the mast. I then checked the sheave which seemed undamaged but appeared to have popped the four rivets securing it to the mast. Finally, as the sun set in a glorious flash of colour, I sat down on the deck and concentrated on how this had happened and a possible solution. The obvious way to sort both was relatively straightforward – a visit to the masthead with the sheave and a couple of new screws/bolts for a thorough inspection. However, Ellen Macarthur I was not and I had promised Shaunagh I would not go aloft unless in dire extremis. Happily this failed to meet that category now everything was down.

Daylight faded quickly and, rather than spend a fruitless hour straining eyes and imagination for a solution, I rigged the boat for the night and went below tired and sweaty. There was nothing I could do until the morning so it made sense to relax. Time for a shower and a drink.

The shower had been a great mood saver during the trip. Because of conditions, for the first few days after leaving Las Palmas I had been unable to use the shower – a soapy wash in such a confined space would have inevitably led to more broken ribs if not also legs and arms – not unlike being in a washing machine on a cold rinse cycle. A cold bucket in the cockpit was as good as it got. I certainly wasn't tempted to follow the example set by one of my icons, Robin Knox-Johnston, when competing in the 1969 Golden Globe award to become (successfully) the first man to sail non-stop around the world. Apparently, he washed and took exercise by diving off the front of his boat, *Suhaili*, completely unattached to it, swimming as fast as he could whilst it slowly overtook him before tucking in behind to grab the stern and climb back aboard. Not my idea of a relaxing wash. After three days of my limited washing the result, as anyone who has sailed for more than two days in wet weather kit will instantly recognise, was the unpleasant experience of wafts of warm air of an increasingly pungent nature exiting the trousers every time I sat down. As the rowing correspondent for *The Guardian* wrote on entering the 1977 Oxford crew's rented house in Hammersmith – *'there*

was a strong smell of wet cabbage and private parts'.
Thus, the first hot shower I had allowed myself after Delta
had finally dissipated on my fourth day out had made me
feel re-born. The salty stickiness and sweaty staleness
sloshed around my feet under the duckboards in a dark
brown scummy liquid as I happily towelled myself dry.
Ever since then I had keenly looked forward to my evening
shower to wash away the P20 sun cream, salt and sweat
of each day.

After supper I sat at the nav station for a while
pondering over the broken sheave, trying to estimate arrival
time and my dwindling diesel supplies. I had enough of
the latter to last but with 750 miles to go it was anybody's
guess as to arrival time. Shaunagh was flying to Barbados
the next day and was going to speak with the marina at
Port St Charles to confirm whether I could slip in and
berth at night without restriction in the event of an arrival
after sunset. After 20 plus days I didn't want to stand off
overnight or get re-routed to the main anchorage further
south at Carlisle Bay off Bridgetown.

To close the day and in an effort to take my mind off
the immediate issues of the broken sheave and the fuel
supply I sat after dinner in the saloon and listened to a
couple of CDs. Throughout the trip I had variously
listened to Peter Ustinov, Billy Connolly and others to
give me a lift. Tonight I decided that with no sign of bad
weather or heavy squalls I should try and relax and enjoy
an evening of appalling humour and another small nip
of Armagnac. Needless to say I probably had one nip
more than I should but I collapsed in helpless laughter

at the refrain in one of Jasper Carrot's songs of, *'I've had trouble passing water ever since I met your daughter'*. Swapping to a Billy Connolly CD I fell about even more at his story of the Queen on a visit to a military hospital where a wire brush and Dettol appeared to be the cure for every ailment. Sad and bad but nonetheless they both cheered me up considerably.

16 Dec – 07:44 GPS – pos: N15°10' | W049°05'

Distance covered in previous 24 hours	116 nm
CL total	2,278 nm
HL total	2,292 nm
+/–	–14 nm

Sometime after midnight the wind picked up. For much of the remainder of the night *Fathom* maintained just under eight knots in force 6–7 NE winds – It was just typical that the ideal wind arrived 12 hours after losing use of the chute. However, I was very grateful to have got the whole sausage down as in such conditions it would have flogged itself and the rig to pieces. As it was, we were having quite a ride in the dark under full main and a double-reefed genoa. By now I had either got braver in terms of carrying more sail and/or had become much more comfortable with the stronger, but more consistent, winds. Having to reef the genoa was irritating but, apart from not wanting to get caught unexpectedly at night by a squall, the genoa still suffered from being blanketed from the wind by the main when running downwind. Boring but easier on the nerves even if the result was a somewhat unpleasant yawing caused by lack of sail balance. I had tried reefing the main and not the genoa but found this combination even less successful. As I lay in my bunk, naked but with a light blanket across my lower half, I listened to and felt *Fathom* finding her own way across the moonlight swell. With the yawing, I just hoped Otto would not be over-stressed.

Lying there in the darkened saloon I realised I would go under the 600 mile marker around midday. That sudden realisation made me smile as, after 19 days and 2,300 miles on my own, it suddenly seemed such a short distance. I also smiled at the thought that today, at about the same time, Shaunagh would fly over me en-route to Barbados and take only one and a half hours to cover a distance that would take me at least another three to four days, especially without the use of the chute. I drifted off into a happy and contented sleep for an hour or so.

After an early breakfast I thought I would have another go at trying to work out exactly what had gone wrong at the masthead. Taking my binoculars I went forward and sat on the deck. At that moment, a small family of five dolphins raced in towards the boat and, instead of lying on my back looking up the mast, I found myself lying on the deck looking over the toe-rail for 20 minutes with my new playmates. The older ones played on the bow-wave competing with one another to get faster and closer to my bow without actually touching it. Every now and again, with an invisible signal between them, they would suddenly break the surface like torpedoes, take sharp breathes and veer off giving way to a mother and small calf. It was enchanting to watch how she then gently coaxed her calf to twist and turn in shorter bursts alongside *Fathom* in a clear lesson to copy the others.

I remembered another time four years earlier when Shaunagh and I had taken the Portsmouth – Bilbao ferry. Half-way across the Bay of Biscay I stood on a side deck and watched a different pod of dolphins appear from nowhere and race to swim alongside the huge steel box of a hull. Being a keen naturalist, it was a sight my father would have loved. For some reason I had taken a £2 coin from my pocket as a form of offering to Neptune on behalf of my father. I threw it high into the air and watched it fall. When it hit the surface I stood for a while as I imagined it sinking slowly beneath me into the dark and cold depths to lie forever in the mud of the sea-bed. To this day I have no idea what impulse made me do that but I find myself quite often thinking of that coin whenever I see dolphins.

After they had gone, I wondered why I had seen so little wildlife – certainly the bad weather had played a part, but I was very disappointed not to have seen more in the quieter moments. The week before leaving the UK I had read some of the emails being sent by individual boats in the ARC fleet during the first few days after they had left Las Palmas. Regular reports of turtles, dolphins, sail fish and even a whale had been posted on the rally site, all of which had whetted my appetite and raised my expectations. As it was, sightings had been very rare and mostly fleeting or distant. The one astonishing fact was that I don't recall a single day when I did not see or was not visited by a bird of some kind – petrels mainly but as I closed Barbados tropic birds started to appear in ones and twos. The distances they must regularly fly is astonishing. Apart from the obvious bad weather I supposed it could have been my mix of Dire Straits, Eminem and Ry Cooder over the cockpit speakers that had discouraged closer inspection; possibly also my lack of a proper bath in 18 days hadn't helped. However, as we got closer to the Caribbean Islands, I hoped more would show up.

Once the dolphins had got bored and disappeared, I rolled over and lay on my back on the deck squinting through the binoculars at my masthead. Slowly I identified each piece of running and standing rigging attached to the mast and finally worked out what had gone wrong – it was entirely my fault. At the masthead there are two halyards (apart from the genoa halyard), one 18 inches or so below the other. I had been using the Cazenove chute in preference to my light-air starburst chute as it was made of stronger material. However, it was also smaller and, as a result, I had been using the lower of the two halyards. This exits the mast via a built-in sheave just above the removable inner-forestay and was clearly for the storm jib. It was designed for vertical tension and not the lateral stress that a chute exerts, especially with the light winds and wrenching conditions of the day before.

The halyard I should have been using exited the mast just above the genoa – after exiting the mast it then appeared to go straight to a block above the swivel for the self-furler. My problem had been that from deck level it was impossible to see what block or fittings were above the genoa swivel. Worried that any fitting would interfere with the genoa I had wrongly decided to be cautious and use a halyard whose fittings were clearly visible. That it had lasted for as long as it had without breaking sooner is a tribute to the quality of the Beneteau/Z spar fittings.

Whilst confident I had identified the reason for the problem I was still a touch unsure about using the higher halyard without seeing what configuration of blocks and halyards hung around at the masthead. When the boat had been rigged on delivery in Barcelona I had been too busy checking the myriad of other electronic, mechanical and technical bits to remember to check the masthead. Various riggers had been up and down the mast since then but I never had. The lesson to learn is to do it yourself or, at the very least, be familiar with everything from stem to stern and masthead to keel.

With the wind dropping to around nine knots I decided that it would take a week to reach Barbados without the chute. Throwing caution to the dropping wind, I dragged the sail bag and chute sheets up to the foredeck once again. Apprehensively, I prepared, hoisted and released the chute. It opened lazily and, once I was back in the cockpit and had tightened the sheet, filled like a soft balloon. I was relieved and delighted to see our speed increase by a whole knot from 2.5 knots to 3.5 knots. Progress!

Four hours later I lowered it with no problems when the wind all but died again. I was doubly relieved at knowing I could use the chute for the rest of the trip but irritated with myself for my stupidity in not having used the correct halyard from the start – one lives, breaks things and then learns!

17 Dec – 09:22 GPS – pos: N14°54' | W051°32'

Distance covered in previous 24 hours	*126 nm*
CL total	*2,404 nm*
HL total	*2,412 nm*
+/–	*–8 nm*

Someone once told me that the wonderful thing about trade-wind sailing is that the winds are so consistent – they were right in a way, I suppose, as it blows a wonderful force 5/6 at night but at 09.00hrs every morning the fan gets turned right down to a very dodgy force 1/2. The previous 24 hours had been typical – we ratcheted up good speed overnight only to spend seven hours during the day wobbling around in a miserable excuse for wind at a speed most pensioners could better on foot. Putting the chute up merely kept us a nose in front of those using zimmer frames.

It's the wrong way round really as with the better wind conditions at night I had been unable to sleep for more than a total of four hours or so as I had to be in the cockpit controlling our speeds. However, during the day I had struggled to stay awake as *Fathom* wallowed listlessly in light winds. Interestingly, whilst frustrating in one sense I did, however, appear to be able to function perfectly normally. Much of that I am sure was to do with being on my own and being able to do things at my own speed and in my own time and space. This I believe now to be one of the great luxuries of solo sailing. I would have to consider very carefully in future whether doing a similar length trip with others would be anything like as enjoyable or companionable. I am, by nature, quite relaxed in my approach to most things, much to Shaunagh's utter frustration and our childrens' huge amusement, but would find having to accommodate others' habits, smells, space and requirements quite demanding. I would also suspect that boredom would set in as any watch routine shared with others creates spare time, which I would find even more frustrating than tiredness. I like other people hugely and am very far from being a misanthrope but confined spaces tend to bring the worst out in people, me included. It's not a risk I would take with many.

However, one of the benefits of short nights is the completely different perspective given to day sailing. Everything seems so much calmer and quieter. I had been either side of a full moon for the past 5 days and it had been beautiful to sit in the cockpit in the hour before dawn with a massive, heart-stopping bacon sarnie and mug of tea. Most mornings I had the moon shining across the open ocean as the first pink flush of dawn pushed over the eastern horizon. In the pre-dawn moonlight I could see a full 360 of the entire horizon and could even have rigged the chute but the beauty of the scene easily overcame lethargy as the reason not to. As the sun burned its way over the horizon in a blaze of colour that pierced the clouds and lit their rims with silver edges I sat and felt the last damp breath of the ocean dawn disappear in the warmth of the coming day. It was an awesome and truly beautiful display of nature.

Such conditions gave me some time to relax and the last two days had allowed me some 'down' time for boat-work and to listen to more of the talking books I had brought with me. I had already finished Bill Clinton (disingenuous but interesting on health care), Andrew Marr (fascinating but enough to put anyone off political journalism) and A Hitchhikers Guide to the Galaxy (can't see what all the fuss was about). I had put off listening to The Life of Pi as everyone said I was nuts to take it with me given the storyline of a shipwreck. However, today I decided that I fancied a nautical theme and that I would listen to the first CD in the set. I was instantly engrossed. I may not have had a zebra or a lion on *Fathom* but I spent most of the day in the liferaft with Pi and his menagerie. It was one of the few days for which I have little recollection of the sailing other than it was comfortable and I experienced no problems with sail changes or conditions. I must have been happy and content.

Being in such a frame of mind, I found myself pondering why my father had found solo sailing disagreeable. He clearly loved the freedom offered by the sea and I wondered whether it was his inability to amuse himself on passage that led to this dislike. He always took himself too seriously and whilst he had a sense of humour he had little obvious sense of the absurd. To me this is an essential part of life. His worst effort many years earlier was when he picked me up, aged 12, from Palma airport in his large commercial van from the nursery garden. It was an old van and on which, emblazoned in large letters down each side, was his advertising slogan 'VIVERO HORTUS'. Sadly, the silencer had long since disintegrated which resulted in a deafening noise and clouds of grey diesel smoke following him wherever he went. As we pulled out of the airport car park we must have looked and sounded like Del and Rodney Trotter. Conversation was almost impossible but with masterful mistiming he took this opportunity to shout me through the facts of life. I had just left hospital two days earlier having been circumcised and was in very real discomfort. The combination of subject matter, noise and pain resulted in my not fully understanding what he was talking about. The bits I did hear froze me to my seat in horror as I could hardly believe my kit would ever recover sufficient shape or size to get involved in any of the activities he seemed to be describing. We hardly said a word to one another for days afterwards.

This inability to gauge occasion seemed a recurrent theme in our relationship. Having said that and having spoken with Clare and Giles, my full sister and brother, I certainly do not feel I was in any way a special case. However, from my point of view, I always felt that whatever I did was completely irrelevant and of no interest to him at all. The only common grounds for a relationship between us were his interests and what he did. I found that more than mildly one-sided and irritating so, for a while, I tried to force him into a reaction, any reaction, to achieve some form of acknowledgement by him of me as an individual. I wrote him a couple of very emotionally charged letters. I was angry, not just for myself but also for Clare and Gi. Strangely for me, they both appeared less concerned but perhaps I just wear my heart on my sleeve more than they do. At any rate, my letters bore no obvious fruits with my father and finally I decided to give up seeking any form of recognition as his son as it was quite obviously a complete waste of time for both of us.

He did tell me a year or so later that he had never regarded me as a son – more as a much younger brother. As he had none of the latter but three of the former I found it quite difficult to understand how he had arrived at this profound conclusion. In the end I gave up trying to understand and just accepted it. Strangely, it was only then that some flicker of a closer relationship emerged as it coincided with Shaunagh and me buying our house near him in Catalunya. By then he had been diagnosed with Parkinson's disease to go with the prostate cancer he had been suffering for the previous 12 years. We knew he was dying and both of us wanted to have one last chance at my getting to know him better.

In his last 18 months he and Jinty, my stepmother, would often drive the 20 minutes or so over to us for a weekend lunch. They would arrive up our rutted track in their old Mercedes with endless dogs barking and yapping on the back seat. It was hardly surprising both were slightly deaf. We would sit on our front terrace overlooking the Gavarre hills covered in olive trees, Mediterranean pine and cork oak eating our local olives and almonds and discussing emotionally 'safe' topics. In those last 18 months he deteriorated slowly to a state where he twice tried to take his own life. Tragically, he failed both times. Dealing with the physical and mental aftermath of each occasion was hard for him and for Jinty. It was clear, however, that knowing how he felt about his condition he was likely to try again. It was getting very tough emotionally for all involved.

After lunch, he and I would usually go for a slow walk around the gardens that Shaunagh and I had been creating since buying the house. Many of the plants had come from the commercial garden he had started in Mallorca in 1967 and which had now become one of the largest on the island. He seemed to take great pleasure from seeing how his seedlings and saplings were developing and he was always careful to compliment me on how well they all looked.

On those walks around the garden he never mentioned his emotions nor the months spent recovering from his two failed suicide attempts. In the end, I took the initiative and wrote one last letter. Why? There were many reasons but I felt he might want to talk to someone about issues surrounding some of his feelings which were possibly too difficult or too unfair to discuss with Jinty. To my surprise he responded.

Over the next few months, he and I had a number of long conversations on our own. They were not always easy but they were always calm and surprisingly free from unnecessary emotion. We covered only a few topics but I got to know him a bit better and certainly witnessed a couple of very private moments when he let his mask slip. I don't think either of us found it comfortable and we were careful to avoid the one or two obvious emotional danger zones. However, in our own ways, we both tried a bit more than in the past.

After one of our weekend lunches, I walked him back to the car. We were on our own. As we slowly walked together I think we both realised this would be the last time we would see one another. When we reached the car, quietly and in that somewhat awkward way he had never quite got used to, we hugged. I held his arm as he started to get in the car and, for some reason, I asked him why dogs licked their balls? He shook his head not knowing the answer and I told him it was because they could. He looked at me for a moment. Then a rumbling laugh, starting deep inside his chest, burst out and he roared with laughter as I hadn't heard him do for so long. He stood there for a while still laughing. When he stopped, we looked briefly but directly into one another's eyes. He turned slowly before lowering himself into the passenger seat and closing the door. As they drove down the drive with the dogs still barking on the back seat he turned round, smiled and waved goodbye.

He committed suicide two days later.

18 Dec – 08:36 GPS – pos: N14°28′ | W054°02′

Distance covered in previous 24 hours	*130 nm*
CL total	*2,534 nm*
HL total	*2,532 nm*
+/–	*+2 nm*

At 06.30hrs I went under the 500 mile marker.

At 08.30 hrs I broke my toe.

I know I broke my toe as it became the size, colour and consistency of a very ripe Victoria plum. I caught it on one of the deck fittings when the chute halyard pulled out of a small open jammer on the mast and the chute started to disappear over the side.

I had just finished breakfast in the cockpit thinking how promising the weather looked. The sea was running with a 9–12ft swell from astern and the wind was steady at around 15–17 knots. I went forward and sat on the foredeck whilst I untied the chute bag from the forward stanchions where I secured it every night. I always rather enjoyed that part of the process as there was something very soothing about the slow lift and fall of the bows as each wave passed under the hull. Every now and again there would be a larger wave that came from a different angle and slapped hard against *Fathom's* side breaking the rhythm and dumping cold sea water over everything on the foredeck including me. That morning, I unpacked the chute from the sail bag and it lay like some vast dead snake across the foredeck. I edged forward and secured the strop from the tack to the stem-head (i.e. the rope from the bottom front-edge of the sail to the front of the boat) and then ran the sheet to the aft winch. I returned to the base of the mast and attached the halyard to the head of the chute and started to hoist the sausage arm over arm to the top of the mast. Once fully up, I pushed the halyard that was now holding the whole sausage aloft into an open jammer on the mast to secure it temporarily whilst I calmly but quickly crawled aft towards the cockpit to take in the 15 metres of slack halyard that lay on the deck. It was then that one of those larger waves caught us broadside. There was a terrific bang as the wave caught the side of the hull and *Fathom* shook from her keel to her masthead. I can't remember whether I heard or saw what happened next as it was so fast – the halyard, yanked out of the open jammer by the shock, raced back aloft whilst the entire chute-in-a-sausage fell back down towards the deck. I could not reach the halyard before the knot on its end thankfully caught in a jammer. By then, the head of the sail had not only fallen to deck level but also been blown outside the stanchions into the sea and was being pulled over the side.

I had not quite reached the cockpit before the wave hit us and so was facing in the wrong direction for any rapid movement. However, realising things were out of control I quickly twisted round to go forward and, as I did so, I felt a short sharp tug and a searing pain as my small toe caught in a deck fitting. I had no time to think but fell to my knees and through watering eyes lurched for a handful of rapidly disappearing chute.

I tried to stay still for a moment to let the pain in my toe subside but I felt myself being dragged along the deck and beginning to loose my grip on the chute as it was inexorably pulled overboard. Struggling painfully to a sitting position I grabbed as much of the chute as remained with both hands and arms and just held on. It stopped going overboard. Rather frantically and slightly optimistically I looked around for another hand. There wasn't one.

The available ones were already fully occupied. Bugger! Matters were, in fact, getting worse – I could see the snuffer was in the water and being dragged backwards by the slow movement of the boat through the water. Gradually, very gradually, it was sliding back up the submerged sausage and releasing the sail. If that happened I would have a real struggle on my hands, especially as it seemed some of the sail had already been sucked under the hull. It was vital to stop that happening and recover the whole sail and snuffer before they became entwined around the keel, propeller and rudder. Should that happen, I would have no choice other than to dive over the side with a knife and cut the whole lot away. Not necessarily an easy or quick operation and certainly not in 17 knots of wind, a 10ft sea and on my own.

My only discernible option was brute strength. For the first 5 minutes, but which felt like 15, it was all I could do to recover six inches of sail every time I heaved. Every now and again I would lose half of that as a wave caught the submerged sail and literally threatened to pull me over the side unless I let some go. At one stage I thought I couldn't hold it any longer. After what felt like the longest tug-of-war in history I managed to get the snuffer onboard and after that it became easier.

It felt like an age before I had the whole kit back safely within the guard-rails – sail, snuffer, sheet and halyard – and when I pulled the final armful on board I collapsed on the deck shaking with physical exhaustion. For 10 minutes I could hardly move. It was only once my muscles had started to recover that I remembered my toe.

Sitting up to examine it I could see straightaway that it was at a bit of an odd angle and was beginning to throb badly. It didn't look terribly nice but then my feet never do. It was also going a rather disgusting colour. However, toes are like ribs and not possible to do much with when damaged so I resigned myself to being very careful not to knock it again and to the fact that it would hurt for a few days. I did at least push it back into roughly the right shape.

Trying to keep my foot away from the acres of sail and sheets that lay all over the deck in a wet mess I leaned against the mast and started the laborious process of unpacking and then untwisting the entire sail, all 450 square feet. I needed to check for any damage as even the slightest tear would split the chute like a zipper if I put it back up again without repairing it. Astonishingly, Lady Luck was smiling on me and the chute was in one piece. I then had to carefully repack it in the snuffer before starting the process all over again and hoisting it aloft. 20 minutes later, undamaged, it was up and working perfectly. It had been a narrow escape from a second potential cock-up with the chute. I was mightily relieved, limped back to the cockpit and stuck my foot in a bowl of sea water and a packet of semi-frozen peas.

Physically, the rest of me was in pretty good nick. The ribs were definitely on the mend although I still couldn't lie on my front and sneezing was to be avoided at all costs. Other than that, the only other casualties seemed to be my hands which, after 21 days at sea and even with wearing sailing gloves, now looked like those on a three-week old cadaver. Much of the skin had been going white and flaking like old blisters such that skin was peeling off my fingers and palms. None of it was painful, it just looked very unattractive and I tried to keep cream on them at night to stop them drying out. What I wasn't quite so sure how to categorise was the beard. I announced when leaving Las Palmas that I would make another attempt at growing one as my last attempt, curiously and somewhat unfairly made when on honeymoon in Egypt with Shaunagh, had looked casually unpleasant. This was partly as I have vitiligo, a skin condition that produces white patches all over my body and face and on which only white hair grows. It was also because we were only away for two weeks. After almost three weeks at sea, however, I had managed an altogether more substantial affair albeit still somewhat blotchy and uneven in colour. I remained unsure as to whether it improved the overall image. Those that have subsequently seen the photos have fallen into two distinct camps – those that immediately said I looked like Sean Connery (thank you all) and those who said it was more of a Billy Connolly look (all of my five children). There was a certain salty-sea doggedness about it but I found it acted too often as an involuntary filter for most eating and drinking activities. For reasons I couldn't fully understand, food no longer passed smoothly between my lips and into my mouth but got lost somewhere between bowl and mouth. More often than not, spoons were full when last seen leaving bowls in front of me but less so when my lips closed around them a nano-second later.

It was some form of gourmet magic. Things were little different with most forms of liquid. They no longer flowed sweetly through my lips but cascaded rather unattractively over lips, chin and chest. The icing on the beard, literally, came with sun block which, once applied, acted as an impenetrable hair gel. The whole gooey ensemble was a hygienists' nightmare. The nightly shower did dislodge most of the larder so that it looked presentable but on the whole it was probably an experiment not to be repeated. On hearing of my beard from Shaunagh, Harry (my stepson) unfairly but very practically suggested I use it as a nursery for transplanting hairs to my bald patch. I knew it wouldn't last once I got onto dry land.

The negative physical aspect I had noticed over the last couple of days was some obvious weight loss, most noticeably in my legs. I had been going up and down the companionway and realised my legs, always solid from years of rowing, were definitely thinner. I suppose I shouldn't have been surprised, as there had not been many opportunities to go for long walks in the last couple of weeks. Conversely, my shoulders and arms had tightened up noticeably with all the manual winching and sheet work. I now looked like a curious hybrid with the upper body of Steve Redgrave and the legs of Kate Moss. An odd combination but, looking on the bright side, preferable to the other way round.

Broken bits and pieces apart, from a sailing perspective today turned out to be a blast – quite the best and fastest downwind sailing of the trip and a new speed record for *Fathom*.

Having checked and raised the chute after the near disaster the wind started to pick up to speeds above those we had seen over the last couple of days. Within an hour it was a solid force 5 with gusts to 21kts, the very top end in my view for flying the chute especially when single-handed. I had also left the double-reefed main up that I had carried overnight. Gusts started to come in at 22–23 knots and *Fathom* took off like something possessed. The next three hours were electrifying – sustained speeds in excess of 10 knots with bursts above 11 knots. The highest I saw (twice) was 11.3 kts. It was exhilarating to sail a 41ft, 7.5 ton displacement boat solo at such speeds like a dinghy zigzagging across, down and occasionally through a three to four metre sea. My hands were clamped to the wheel as I knew that getting back to the foredeck to douse the chute was not very practical. However, the raw energy and excitement was not something I wanted to turn off and was busy yeehawing my way very loudly across that particular part of the ocean. Thankfully there was still no-one out here to witness this enthusiastic but rather sad behaviour by a part-clad 50 year old. For aficionados of Dr. Strangelove, I felt just like the pilot astride the H bomb as he manually triggered the jammed release mechanism.

With some relief I noticed the wind starting to drop in the early afternoon. Lack of sleep, intense concentration and lack of food is a bad combination so to save giving myself an early heart attack I dropped the chute. Once it was down, bagged and tied to the guard rails I sat wearily and sweatily on the foredeck examining how much slower we were going and considered putting it straight back up again. Lethargy won.

A couple of hours before sunset I saw a yacht three miles ahead of me but, again, couldn't raise them on VHF. On radar we seemed to be on parallel headings and I thought I stood a chance of catching them the next day if conditions allowed me to use the chute again all day. I also noticed the radar shadow of what looked like a freighter about 10 miles ahead; it was beginning to look rather crowded in this part of the ocean and that meant we were getting close. With a sudden pang of unexpected disappointment I saw the computer was now estimating an arrival time in Port St Charles before closing time Tuesday, only two days away. I should have been more excited but, instead, felt a strange sense of being robbed of any pleasure at the realisation that we were entering the home straight. It was almost as if I had been mugged.

At sunset, with another large squall coming up behind me, I gybed onto a port tack to avoid the possibility of an early evening roughing-up. The wind had also gone easterly, forcing me too far north. In yet another very mucky and increasingly disturbed sea I stayed on this tack overnight with what felt like very little sleep. This wasn't helped by knowing that, sometime before dawn, I would gybe back onto starboard tack to avoid heading too far south. It was frustrating to be this close and not be able to sail in a straight line.

19 Dec – 08:50 GPS – pos: N13°46′ | W056°15′

Distance covered in previous 24 hours	153 nm
CL total	2,687 nm
HL total	2,652 nm
+/–	+35 nm

Tiredly putting the kettle on at 04.45hrs I realised this was probably going to be my last full day at sea. The computer was still estimating an evening arrival the next day in Port St Charles based on the existing conditions and, whilst dark outside, conditions seemed stable enough. However, I still decided to wait for dawn before making a call on using the chute as the sea was still running at 12 feet plus and that always provided a degree of adrenalin for an interesting hoist.

Although short on sleep, I began to think about arrival and to try and make myself relax properly for only the second or third time since arriving in the Canaries over three weeks ago. This was a fatal mistake – I exploded a shackle on one of the two main sheet blocks when gybing just before dawn – and entirely my fault again through in-attention and slack over-confidence. I could not immediately see what had happened as, in the dark, all I had heard was a sharp bang after the boom had swung over my head and the subsequent sound of what sounded like bits of metal falling onto the coach-roof. Limping because of the toe and scrabbling around on hands and knees I located a number of metal parts that had slid onto the deck and worked out what had broken. Looking at the boom I saw that the main sheet was in an extremely precarious position and only being held in place by the remnants of the shattered shackle jammed into a block. Rapidly making the cockpit a cat's cradle of warps to hold the boom and main (still up) so as to free the main sheet, I replaced the missing shackle with a spare from the spares locker. When finished, I was rather pleased to have made the running repairs in those conditions with no loss of speed.

Unlike the rest of this last week, I did not get the chute up straight after breakfast as the wind and sea state were still quite boisterous. I delayed throughout the morning and went for the hoist just after lunch as I thought the wind had steadied enough at a full force 5 although the sea was running at 12–14 feet. Within minutes of releasing the chute I became concerned whether I had made the right decision – I was tired and realised I was mentally marginally off the pace – but the boat took off slaloming fast and almost drunkenly across whole hills and valleys of water. I felt immediately apprehensive and, for the first time in 22 days, I questioned my judgement with an unaccustomed level of unease. Strangely, with hindsight, I then did the one thing I should not have done and flipped Otto on and went below. Anything more stupid would be hard to imagine as conditions were very borderline for using a cruising chute and the one thing that was needed was an eye on the wave patterns to avoid broaching. It was almost as if I didn't want to know what was happening in the cockpit. I fiddled with the log and the instruments for a while before realising that I was being a fool and returned to the cockpit to take control. As it happened, for the next three hours I had an exhilarating time at the wheel with the adrenalin pumping me back to full attention and concentration as we consistently maintained speeds around 10 knots. That final burst got me to below the 100 mile marker but left me feeling pretty drained.

For what I hoped would be the last time, an hour before sunset I rigged the boat for the night. I dropped and stowed the chute, reefed the main and ran the preventer from the end of the boom to the amid-ship cleat. Clearing up in the cockpit and washing the accumulated clutter from lunch in the galley sink I contemplated an evening of quiet reflection. I showered, cooked a final supper and then took a glass of wine into the cockpit as the butter yellow moon rose gradually over the horizon. These evening moments were perhaps the only times I felt myself relax to any meaningful extent. They never lasted for very long as tiredness usually forced me below after a long day of physical and mental activity. I had been surprised by how little time I seemed to have each day and really treasured the 30 minutes or so I stole when the weather had allowed. Six months before leaving I had stockpiled about a dozen books I longed to read along with some DVDs that I fully intended to watch to help relax and pass what I had thought would be long hours on my own. I remember being somewhat surprised that Malcolm had laughed loudly when I mentioned my literary intentions the night before I left Las Palmas. He told me I would have little time in which to indulge such fantasies and I laughed equally loudly back at his absurd comment – there were

24 hours in every day and I couldn't possibly be occupied for all of them. How wrong I was.

I had little time to disappear into a book. Instead I had disappeared into an ocean and experienced something that no book could ever describe adequately or any writer, poet or artist paint in words or colours. The books remained on the shelves, the DVDs in their boxes. In their place my mind was completely overwhelmed by the awesome beauty and scale of my surroundings and the restless landscape of the ocean. I had no need for any form of escape from my surroundings as I had gone beyond my imagination and entered a magical world I had never seen before. I felt utterly free.

20 Dec – 10:22 GPS – pos: N13°26' | W058°48'

Distance covered in previous 24 hours	142 nm
CL total	2,821 nm
HL total	2,797 nm
+/–	+24 nm

I had hoped my final night would be one of quiet rest and calm reflection. What a fool. Three lumping, soaking, blowing, slapping squall lines hit us in rapid succession from 04.00hrs and so the night was a short one again – it would have been a pity to have broken the habit I suppose. Strangely, an hour after dawn and with less than 50 miles to go, the weather cleared up completely and I watched the squalls marching ahead of us towards Barbados. I was on the final home run in bright blue skies and a dark blue ocean. As if from nowhere, two tropic birds appeared and circled the masthead before taking up positions either side as if to escort me the final distance. They were the first birds I had seen other than petrels since just before Delta and were a delight to watch sliding and gliding across the air stream coming off my sails.

Before starting, I had tried to imagine so often how I would feel at this point and on sighting land. During the trip I had, conversely, never once let myself consciously anticipate those feelings. I had considered this bad luck and, apart from anything else, I had never experienced the least desire to finish faster than I was going to. When I did first think I could see a low in-determinate shadow on the horizon, at 08.17 that morning, and held my binoculars steady long enough to realise Barbados was in sight, I recall no particular sense of elation or overwhelming relief. Somehow it almost felt the opposite and I recalled the saying – *'there are two terrible things for man: not to have fulfilled his dream, and to have fulfilled it'*.

Quietly and calmly, I started to check off in my head the various things I needed to do to ensure our arrival was tidy and efficient. It felt strangely normal and as if I had done this a hundred times before. I wasn't dis-appointed not to feel more excited any more than I felt displeased not to have been a day or so faster than my father's time of 23 days. All things considered, I was pleased to have equalled his time given that he had motor-sailed for 95% of his crossing and with the company of others. Additionally, the weather I had experienced en-route by popular experienced opinion had been the most mixed for many years. However, I did wonder why I felt balanced so finely between being over-whelmed and under-whelmed.

I partly blame technology. In my father's day, and up until quite recently, the art of navigation relied on a navigator's skill with the sextant. He always said his best moment was on seeing land, closely followed by establishing whether he was anywhere close to where he thought he was. I just turn the chartplotter on and push a button to show where I am anywhere in the world to within one metre. Not quite the same really. As I got up that morning, I knew with certainty I was only 49.6 miles from my waypoint on the northern tip of Barbados and that I would see land sometime over the next four hours. My father must have experienced entirely different emotions of huge excitement, after 22 days at sea, along with uncertainty and hope that nothing had caused his calculations to be wrong. Seeing land for him must have given a tremendous mixed feeling of relief and satisfaction and a very visual confirmation of his skills. For me, it merely confirmed that my batteries were charged.

I also partly blame my self-control. For 23 days I had kept a very strong rein on my emotions. Those deep waters had only been ruffled when unexpectedly affected by events such as the bad weather and being followed, or by the raw beauty of my surroundings. I vividly remember a couple of occasions climbing sleepily into the cockpit at dawn and being completely overwhelmed by the delicate intricacy of every colour hanging in the sky as the first glimmers from the distant sun started to warm the night sky and push it back over the far horizon. Or the trails of phosphorescence tumbling in our wake as *Fathom* powered across a sea bathed in silver moonlight. Or the sudden appearance of dolphins clicking and squeaking as they rode our bow wave. Even the morning after the storm, the ocean had displayed breath-taking elemental beauty and a primitive natural power. Those had been extraordinary moments to experience which had forced me out of my self-control for a short while and given me intense feelings of exhilaration. However, they were unexpected moments and died as the sun rose to bleach the sky or the dolphins swam away to leave me once more alone and in control of my environment. Seeing land was not unexpected, it just became a log entry.

I called Shaunagh on the satellite phone. Peculiarly, given I was now in sight of land and 'safe', we had our first small lack of understanding. I had thought that she and Mona (in whose wonderful house, Jackson Heights on Sandy Lane, and with whom we were staying along with cousin Wilf)) would rush impatiently to some headland. There they would watch for *Fathom* to appear out of the vastness of the ocean under full sail thrusting the waves aside and surfing down the face of the trans-Atlantic rollers that had been born off the African coast thousands of miles behind us. I had created a wonderful mental image of my wife, hair blowing in the gusting wind, standing on the desolate headland with the surf pounding against the base of the cliffs beneath her feet whilst gulls circled above calling her to my imminent safe arrival. As it was, to my disappointment, they had gone to a beach-restaurant on the other side of the island by the marina. So, no pounding surf, no circling gulls, no windblown wife just *Fathom* and I left to make the final run-in on our own. Admittedly it was Mona's idea and more practical but, momentarily, I felt cheated as I knew that by the time they saw us, *Fathom* would be festooned with fenders and under engine with all sails packed away no longer the sleek and beautiful ocean crosser I had shared 23 extraordinary days with. She would look like any other boat out for a day sail and I had wanted it to be different, to be seen at our best under full sail. After what we had been through I was disappointed for both of us.

An hour or so later, resigned to our arrival and with individual coastline details beginning to be visible to the naked eye, I started to tidy up above and below decks. Although I had kept the boat well tidied, I needed to start packing away those items no longer required and find those that would be necessary for berthing. Whilst retrieving mooring lines from the cockpit locker I glanced behind me and, once again, saw a boat coming over the horizon – only the fourth in the last 2,900 miles. This one was a large motor yacht and had obviously come over from the Canaries or the Cape Verde islands and had been steaming at 10 knots for the last 10 days. As she drew level she passed 300 yards to port with no decrease in speed and with three crew clearly visible on deck. No-one waved back as I raised my hands in greeting.

Feeling somewhat unloved by the lack of acknow-ledgment by my fast-overtaking neighbours, I found myself instead reflecting on the generosity all those friends and colleagues who had given so much support with their time, energy, advice and donations. With Port St Charles some fifteen miles or so away I quickly went below and sent my penultimate email to the website. I ended it with my favourite few lines from Hilaire Belloc as a thank you to all of them:

> *From quiet homes and still beginnings*
> *Out to undiscovered ends*
> *There's nothing worth the wear of wining*
> *Save laughter and the love of friends.*

Three hours later, as my depth gauge abruptly sprang into life rounding the northern headland a mile offshore after 23 days' silence, it finally sank in that I was almost there. As I slowly came round the lee of the island I spent much of the time with my nose in the air trying to pick up the scent of land and human habitation. After 23 days I assumed it would be a wonderful mix of warm earthy smells mixed with exotic plants and dry vegetation as this was the one thing my father wrote longingly about when making landfall – the excitement of smelling land for the first time after a long ocean crossing:

And so, 23 days after we left Las Palmas we caught the smudge on the horizon that was Barbados and not so long afterwards as we rounded the southern end about a couple of miles out to sea, the land smells assailed us, a tropical earthy smell, intensely strong after a month spent at sea.

Disappointingly, in the strong breeze that was blowing,

nothing carried the mile or so across the sea. After being alone for so long I felt somewhat short-changed not to sense those first faint hints of a foreign land.

I dropped and bagged the main, tidied up the last few loose ends in the cockpit and pulled all the fenders out of the aft locker where I had stowed them. They had lain there undisturbed since leaving the entrance of the Muelle Desportivo in Las Palmas and it seemed so strange to be taking them out again, almost as if I had only just put them away. I suppose it was only then that I realised it was over. After two years of living daily with every aspect of completing a solo transatlantic my 23 days seem to have become no more than 23 hours. I was tired and wanted to stop. Yet I also wanted my fragile world to continue for much longer. It was a bitter sweet moment and I realised why Bernard Moitessier had written about wanting to 'save his soul' by abandoning the Golden Globe in 1969 when leading the race and to carry on sailing around the world. The open ocean has a siren call and sings and whispers seductively to anyone who loves the freedom she offers. But for most she is a mistress not a wife and, sooner or later, must always be put aside. Tying the last fender slowly onto the guardrail I bade my own farewell of her for the moment and quietly gave thanks for a safe arrival.

Running down the coast about half a mile offshore under genoa, I suddenly remembered that I had to find and hoist my bright yellow Q flag for customs to denote I was arriving from abroad. Never having done this before I had a sudden attack of insecurity as to which spreader it should be worn on. I had visions of getting it wrong and rather than denoting a new arrival I would be signalling that I was suffering from yellow fever. As it happened, I either guessed correctly or customs were understanding of tired soloists.

Having sorted out what I thought was the last requirement for an orderly arrival, I began to anticipate the moment I saw Shaunagh for the first time. Hardly surprisingly she had been feeling likewise sitting at the lunch table on the restaurant veranda. She had been trying to recognise *Fathom* from the other boats sailing along the coastline aided and abetted by Wilf. Regrettably, both their boat recognition skills were somewhat shy of the mark and apparently a couple of wildly enthusiastic false starts were made along the beach with madly waving arms and lots of shouting at what turned out to be mildly surprised local skippers. By the time they did identify *Fathom* correctly a more cautious approach had been adopted. Wilf stood on the end of the pier with his hands in his pockets and shouted 'It's Wilf. Well done!' in that peculiarly understated British way. Next to him, Shaunagh did mini-skips on the spot and seemed to me from the cockpit to be telling everybody I was her husband and could they please make room for me to dock.

For the final time I started the engine and for the first time in 20 days since being followed off the African coast engaged the propeller. Shaunagh and I had both separately spoken with the marina and she shouted over confirming that I should moor alongside the fuel jetty which lay, slightly to my alarm, immediately behind four of the largest super-yachts I had ever seen. Each was festooned with fenders that were bigger than my inflatable tender. Gingerly and gently, in front of a growing audience whose curiosity had been kindled by Shaunagh's shore-side aerobics, I swung *Fathom* slowly past the big boats, engaged reverse and as I drew level with the jetty threw my mooring lines ashore. Several hands grabbed them mid-air, slipped them through mooring rings and held them out for me as *Fathom* gently came alongside. I slowly cleated each one off, went to the cockpit and killed the engine.

I had arrived – at 15.37 hrs local time on Tuesday 20th December 2006 exactly 23 days, 9 hours and 55 minutes after casting off from Las Palmas.

20 Dec continued – 19:47 N13°15' | W059°38' Port St Charles Marina

Distance since dawn	*54 nm*
CL total	*2,875 nm*
HL total	*2,851 nm*
+/–	*+ 24 nm*
Phew!	

CHAPTER 4

BARBADOS

That one word, Phew, was sent on its own as my final email. It summed up so succinctly all my feelings as I tied up on the fuel jetty. I was subsequently told by many friends and family that they felt short-changed by its abruptness on the website. However, I felt not dissimilar on my arrival and it did reflect quite accurately my reaction at the time. It was more an expression of bewilderment than relief. It was extraordinary quite how abruptly I departed planet Ocean and landed on planet Earth. Even up to the last half mile I was happily in my own little world, confident in all that was needed and reliant on no-one. As I rounded the breakwater my fragile solo world was shattered by immediate re-entry into the ordered way of life. Lines went ashore, crews on other boats had fended off, Customs, Health, Immigration and marina officials all had to be dealt with whilst family and friends crowded round to help and hug. It seemed a maelstrom of people.

I can now recall much of the next hour but, at the

time, remember feeling I was struggling somewhat. Immediately I had tied off the mooring lines and springs I stepped ashore and then seemed to spend rather too much time speaking to someone who handed me an ice cold beer before embracing my wife. This could have caused something of a diplomatic family incident had Shaunagh not been equally punch drunk to see me back on land. Somehow we sorted ourselves out, hugged one another fiercely and then, more gently, quietly smiled into one another's eyes. That was a great moment.

From then on Shaunagh took control as she tells me I was almost completely ga-ga. Things certainly seemed suddenly to go into slow motion. Signing all the immigration, health and customs forms in the very smart Customs & Immigration building next to the main jetty she had to stand behind me and help me complete all the official forms as I sat with my tongue almost hanging out of my mouth with concentration. I recall it all just feeling so foreign, sitting and copying the forms out in duplicate and making polite conversation with the charming officials. Three Swedes had arrived earlier that morning from Las Palmas after a 20 day crossing having waited in the Canaries for three days after I had left to allow Delta to blow through. We criss-crossed one another in the whitewashed corridors and they looked at me as if I was a simple child – an impression I probably reinforced by permanently smiling at them inanely. None of it seemed to make much sense. All I wanted to do was get *Fathom* onto a proper berth, tidy up the last bits I had not already completed, get the electric shore line hooked up and then sit with Shaunagh over a large drink and savour the moment.

That evening, after that longed-for bath in which I sat with childlike pleasure, Shaunagh, Mona, Wilf, Pierre Luigi (a friend of Mona's staying for Christmas) and I sat round the dinner table on the outside terrace in the warm evening air overlooking her garden. In the distance through the trees in which the monkeys were still shouting at one another I could see the ocean. It felt very strange not to be preparing to set the sails for the night, rig the preventer and cook myself something to eat. As it was, we had the most wonderful dinner of flying fish, salad and fresh tropical fruit all washed down with chilled champagne.

After dinner, longing to lie in a bed that had cotton sheets and didn't lurch, rattle and roll, we said our good-nights and slowly climbed the stairs to our bedroom. Shaunagh was in bed first as I became rather preoccupied in the bathroom examining the beard I had grown over the previous 23 days and trying to decide if I liked it or not. Wiping away the blob of toothpaste that was lodged, like an albino fly in a spider's web, half way down my chin I decided to leave that decision until the morning. With weary limbs, and having averaged little more than 4 ½ hours sleep a night for the last three weeks, I went to climb into bed. Pulling back the sheet I was halted mid pull by an unexpectedly steely expression from Shaunagh. I was informed politely but firmly that if I wished to use the bed that night The Beard must go. What?! She was adamant and said she would feel as if she was in bed with a stranger if I didn't remove it. Personally, I couldn't have given a monkey's at that stage who she was in bed with so long as I could get into one too. However, that look told me all I needed to know. I insisted on a brief photo session to record for the children and scrap-book the only proper beard I am ever likely to grow and then, with a blunt razor, painfully obliterated the offending article.

I lay in bed for a while in the stillness of the darkened bedroom. Next to me Shaunagh fell quickly asleep in the knowledge I was with her and safe. I was too tired and my feelings too befuddled to enjoy the moment fully and I found my mind rambling over a landscape of odd and misshaped thoughts. Some were reflections, some were questions and some were incomplete memories from other lives. They all blended into a strange tangle of memories that dragged me slowly towards sleep. It was nice to let go, to let my mind relax and find its own way now finally released from permanent standby. I rolled onto my side and realised with surprise my ribs no longer hurt – my mind and body already seemed to be moving on from the last 23 days. I slept.

We stayed with Mona at Jackson Heights for the next five days over Christmas. In the first few days everything felt slightly strange and I realised I needed to recharge not only *Fathom's* batteries but mine as well. Mona was, as always, a wonderful hostess and made sure we could relax and have time to ourselves. Alan Godsal, my godfather and Best Man at my parents' wedding, had done likewise 42 years earlier for my father and Jinty.

When Alan generously arranged for Shaunagh and me to have dinner at Cobblers Cove (he was a founding owner of the Hotel) it felt very strange for history to be repeating itself. On arrival at dinner I was presented with a magnum of champagne and a hand-written card from him saying 'Well done but I still think you are nuts'. It was a lovely and generous touch especially as I knew he was unwell. Sitting on the covered veranda by candle-light, overlooking the ocean and with the gentle sound of waves washing up the beach, I wondered how much had changed since my father had arrived 42 years earlier.

Over the next five days the weather stayed fine and between visits to the boat to prepare her for the return voyage Shaunagh and I went for long walks on our own just enjoying being together again. Most mornings we ended up detouring to the beach for a swim. I remember on the first such visit, 24 hours after I had arrived, how strange it felt just to walk into the sea. I found myself silently fighting a strange resistance to do so even though I was on a beach surrounded by many others. Normally, I love any form of swimming but I had spent so long during the last three weeks in a mantra-like frame of mind about the dangers of being in the water that it now felt completely unnatural to walk into it voluntarily. My other strange memory was catching myself looking at the sky continually trying to read the clouds for signs of a weather change. For the whole crossing I had been utterly depen-dant on the wind and had got used to monitoring constantly what conditions were ahead and behind me. In the last week I had lost count of the occasions I had watched and timed squall lines in both directions as if crossing a road and avoiding traffic. Throughout the trip, apart from the sea, the sky had been the most constantly changing element in an otherwise featureless view limited only by the all-encircling horizon. In most ways the sky had become my principal form of information and entertainment and some of my very best memories are still of what I had seen above me during both day and night. This must be the case for many long distance sailors and I try to remember that today but all too rarely examine the sky again as I did on that trip.

We returned to London on Boxing Day flying first class with Virgin Atlantic. I had never flown first class before but had felt that in the event of a safe arrival such comfort would be one of our rewards. Once we had taken off and had finished dinner the lights were dimmed and the seats were converted to flat beds. Shaunagh settled down with her duvet and pillow and went to sleep.

I sat for a long while looking out of the window. I found myself searching for the surface of the dark ocean many thousands of feet below me. With all the physical and mental strains of the journey over I had, at last, some quiet time in which to reflect how lucky and enormously fortunate I was to have completed the trip. I did not feel lucky or fortunate just to have arrived safely. I also felt deeply privileged to have experienced the solitude and vastness of the open ocean. In the remainder of my life I doubt I will do something capable of creating such an intensity of feeling more than once or twice again. I am sure my isolation had only emphasised such feelings, the good as well as the bad, but I had not expected that to happen. In Las Palmas I had set out to achieve nothing more than a safe crossing on my own and had purposefully avoided seeking a cause or anticipating how I might feel or react. Now, in the dimmed lights of the cabin, I wondered whether amongst all the emotions it had stirred up I had been searching for more than just that challenge.

I had followed in my father's watery footsteps and started off using his journey merely as a 23 day benchmark for my own. However, as I had gone deeper into the ocean and further into self-imposed isolation I had found myself looking increasingly for comparisons between my feelings and his. I was very aware that a large gap existed in my memories of him in the years immediately after he and my mother divorced in 1963. In the following two years he completely disappeared from my life whilst he sailed from England to Australia. By following some of his voyage on my own I wondered whether I was trying to recover part of those missing years or at least gain a better understanding of him as an individual. It was T S Eliot who wrote:

> *We shall not cease from exploration*
> *And the end of all our exploring*
> *Will be to arrive where we started*
> *And know the place for the first time*

In the darkened cabin I had no ready answers. In the end, although his shadow had never felt far away my father had remained like the horizon – a permanent illusion of where the ocean meets the sky. In those extraordinary 23 days, no matter how far I travelled, he never came any closer.

Ultimately, I think life is less complex and I'm not so convinced there always needs to be a reason for doing something. My fathers' transatlantic crossing was a public journey away from a type of life in England. It enabled him to reject, physically and mentally, that which he saw as holding little of value for him. Like mountaineers setting out to climb new peaks, I did it for the more straightforward (but no less selfish reason) – just to see if I could. Did trying to delve any deeper into the motives that brought me to follow him bring any greater satisfaction or understanding? I don't think so. It possibly helped me to understand that my relationship with him had depended almost solely upon my input rather than his. When he died I felt no personal loss as I felt unable to mourn someone I never knew.

I looked out through the small perspex window by my elbow into the darkness and watched the flash of our wing-tip navigation lights. I found myself wondering if there was any yachtsman thousands of feet below us looking up at the same small bright flashes, as I had a week earlier, reassured to see he was not completely alone. I hoped so.

With unexpected abruptness I suddenly realised I had missed my family and that I was going home. I was going home on a commercial jet at 36,000 feet with 320 others. It would only take 8 hours to cover almost the same distance it had taken me three weeks to sail. This journey though was in stark and noisy contrast to the beauty and solitude of my days in the Atlantic. As I gazed back down into the blackness beneath me it felt so unnatural to be retracing my watery track unable to feel the wind and roll of the sea, unable to see all the stars and the moon or to taste the damp and salty breath of the ocean.

It took me a long time to get to sleep.

CHAPTER 5

AGAIN?

Those who dream by night in the dusty recesses of their minds wake in the day to find that it was vanity: but the dreamers of the day are dangerous men, for they may act their dream with open eyes, to make it possible.

T E Lawrence

Since the trip I have been asked often if I would do it all again. To a great extent I went off on an unknown adventure and having done it once would there be any novelty left for a repeat? Would I not just be apprehensive of the downsides of tiredness and bad weather without the upside of the unknown?

For me the answers are very straightforward. I have never done anything so completely self-fulfilling before in my life. Neal Paterson, a competitor in the 1994 BOC Round the World Challenge described it as finding .... *'a type of freedom you find only in your mind or soul'*. Rowing for Great Britain in the under-18 World Championships in 1972 and 1973 and in the Boat race in 1975 and 1977 were great moments (I ignore of course the birth of my three children as Sophia, my eldest daughter, so delicately but pointedly mentioned on reading my first draft!). However, they come second to the raw emotions evoked by a solo transatlantic.

Why? I think largely it is to do with being utterly alone and dependent upon no-one. In rowing, to win races at international level you learn to coax, bully and push yourself to and beyond the limit of mental and physical exhaustion. Winter training was all about learning that the mind gives up more easily and quickly than the body. No matter how exhausted we all felt at the end of training, we learned we could always produce another aggressive burst of power. However, we could not have trained like that alone. That was the way Dan Topolski and the training team pummelled the Oxford crews in the 1970s and 1980s and the reason Cambridge lost 14 consecutive Boat Races. The coaches, especially Dan, made us individually believe in dominating other crews through exercising absolute mental and physical control but as a single unit. For the transat, in all the training and during the actual trip I felt myself reverting inexorably towards the same state of mental control. The big difference was the tempo. For each mile of the 4¼ mile Boat Race the crew trained and rowed together over 500 miles in winter training, a total of almost 2,500 miles. Whilst the transat was 2,900 miles it was not a 20 minute concentrated explosion of mind and body over 4¼ miles of tidal river. This difference meant that my transat training had not been as an endless series of exhausting daily outings as it had been for the Oxford crews between November and March. It had been more graduated in anticipation of the trip taking over three weeks. At 50 I realised I could only get some way back to Boat Race physical fitness levels. However, to get across the Atlantic on my own and in one piece I knew I did need to redis-cover the same mental fitness. There would be no coach on the river bank, no minibus to take me back to college and a cooked dinner, no immediate shoulder to lean on when it got difficult and no crew member who I knew was in the same pain bubble as me. I was coach, cook, confidant and crew all rolled into one and I could only blame or congratulate myself. The single fact of being alone did not make me feel vulnerable at all but acted unexpectedly instead as a wonderful release for my emotions and sense of freedom.

Once I had cleared Delta my emotional genie was gradually freed from the bottle. I don't think now I would ever want to return it.

LESSONS TO LEARN

For many, a transatlantic crossing will be the pinnacle of their sailing lives. For others it is just the start. Whichever it may be, there are always lessons to learn no matter how many nautical miles under the belt. I belong to the school of thought that if you can sail for eight hours without any cause for concern you can technically sail quite competently across oceans. The main differences are the equipment needed and the manner of approach, mental and physical. These two points relate directly to experience in handling situations under pressure, knowing the boat and her capabilities and the level of individual preparation.

Before I left Las Palmas, I had sailed a variety of my own boats ranging from a 17ft gaffer to a 41ft sloop over the previous 10 years, clocking up some 6,000 nautical miles along the southern coast of England and the wilder stretches of the Irish Atlantic coast. Not a lot really. I had twice taken my second gaffer (24ft) from Plymouth to Galway via the Fastnet Rock but, even so, the longest ever solo I had done before departing Las Palmas on my 23 day transatlantic crossing was a 42-hour crossing from Spain to Sardinia. Not much either.

However, I would never have contemplated doing the trip if I had felt uncertain. It's a long way to go if you are not sure. I hope I was never over-confident and spent hours planning what-if scenarios in my head. From that came a list of what I think were sensible guidelines for me and which, after the trip, I re-examined closely to see if further lessons could be learned. In no particular order of importance the below, for me, are the most significant;

Fitness

Without question this is one of the most important, especially if you're going solo. Age is immaterial, as Robin Knox-Johnston proved in the 2007 Velux 5 Oceans Challenge. To cope with the stress and tiredness of solo sailing a high level of physical fitness is essential. I trained for 10 months 3 to 4 nights a week and additionally, in the summer months, bicycled a total of 50 minutes every day to and from my office in the City. It was bloody hard work. However, I did get immense pleasure from feeling my body, 25 years after my last Boat Race, start to toughen up properly again. Physical fitness also unquestionably improved my mental strength in absorbing lack of sleep on the trip. It also considerably improved my self-confidence in dealing with the physical challenges of sailing.

Know your boat

Every boat will have her own idiosyncrasies. Knowing a boat well will enable any skipper and/or crew to manage the maximum amount from the boat with the minimum of unnecessary stress. That is not the same as pushing the boat to the maximum. On reflection, I spent the majority of my daily mental focus on an almost paranoid level of making absolutely sure that every small or large thing I did was relevant, safe and effective. For example, I reefed down almost every night and carried less sail than I needed for the conditions. I also put a preventer on the boom *every* night so that I could sleep with relative peace of mind. I knew I was underpowered but it ensured *Fathom* and I looked after one another well.

Likewise, I did considerable research whilst buying *Fathom* to establish in my mind what the best sail configuration was for any given set of conditions. The third reef was invaluable and I frequently thanked the Frenchman whose Beneteau I looked at in Marseilles for passing this nugget on to me. He had taken his boat to Argentina and back with only the standard two reefs and cursed most of the way back. A long way to curse, even in French. Conversely, Graham and the return crew found the removable inner forestay and storm jib equally essential on the way back but, interestingly, best when the jib sheets were led through the chute blocks *behind* the winches before being led on to them.

The experience of going through Delta with *Fathom*

lying 130 degrees off the wind was not something any manual could have told me. In many ways I was just very lucky as I had considered trailing warps. Whilst that would probably have been fine, *Fathom* has a very large open cockpit and I would certainly have been pooped more than once. In future, under such conditions again I would not hesitate to prefer bare poles. Small details perhaps, but learning from and listening to the boat will more often than not tell you what is best.

Check your boat

Alongside idiosyncrasies there will always be the potential weaknesses. No matter whether the boat is old or new, custom or mass-produced, all boats will have them. Take enough time before any long trip offshore to get to know what they are. Once offshore, listen constantly to what the boat is saying and 'walk' the boat *every* day to check for any sign of weakness, looseness, damage or any other early indication of trouble.

This means getting to know every inch of the boat from stem-head to lazarette, from keel to masthead. I dropped a clanger on this one by never going up my own mast before leaving. As a consequence I was unsure as to what configuration I had at the masthead, hence, my stupidity in using the wrong halyard for the cruising chute. This was such an easily avoidable error and one that could have had serious consequences if the broken sheave had cracked the mast. Likewise, my electrical problems turned out to be a dud battery. I had a bank of three in parallel, one of which was almost dry. I had asked for and paid in full for a battery service from the Nauticmar agent in L'Estartit and assumed he had done the job. He hadn't and I didn't check. I was lucky to avoid a fire or damage to the other two batteries. Having said all of the above, I knew before I left that there were bound to be problems – there always are. In my case, most were my fault. However, it is possible to create the best opportunity to enjoy a crossing by minimising problems through thorough checking.

Mental preparation

Like fitness, finding the right mental approach is essential. However, unlike fitness, I found this something for which one could do little in preparation. Never having sailed across an ocean before I had no practical experience on which to build any expectations. However, I knew this element would be one of the three main challenges. As the months went past and I got closer to departure day, I found myself increasingly harking back to my rowing days. Many people say that rowing is one of the toughest endurance team sports. I would partially disagree and say whilst tough it is not a team sport but an individual one. Even if you are sitting in an eight-oared boat with seven others, they may just as well be on another planet as all you see is the back of the bloke in front of you. Even then that sight is only glimpsed through a semi-conscious haze of pounding heart, screaming lungs and agonised legs and arms. Painful though it is, anyone who has known the agony and ecstasy of racing and winning will have learned a high degree of mental toughness. For myself, and the few I have kept up with from those days, this became a part of our characters and is still there today, mostly well hidden under a mound of expense account lunches and soft living. As the Good Book says, the mind is willing but the flesh is weak (so, see **Fitness** as above!).

Tiredness

The Bad One. No matter how good you think you are, tiredness will lead to inattention, even if only momentary. That is as short as it takes to make a potentially fatal mistake. I thought I had clipped on during bad weather when I went forward to bag the main, only to find I had clipped both ends of my lifeline to my safety harness. Twice I had been swung over the side of the boat clutching the boom and I count myself lucky my broken ribs were sufficiently mended not to make me loose my grip. Lack of attention may only happen once on a trip . . . but it will happen.

Most long distance sailing authors have written of the time it takes to establish a rhythm once at sea. Three to five days seems to be the spread, subject to weather conditions and personal characteristics. I would agree with that and believe it is something to do with reaching a level of relative tiredness that forces an adjustment to personal energy levels. It felt somewhat like reaching a cruising altitude when flying and, once achieved, the energy output became easier and less tiring. There were still air pockets, some quite large, but these only seemed to cause immediate distraction and little after-effect.

Tiredness, however, is as bad as you let it become and most times I found I was able to manage my mental and physical energy levels well. My average sleep at night was around five to five and a half hours taken in 45 minute to one hour bursts. Somewhat surprisingly, I never once had to use an alarm clock other than the early morning immediately after being followed. Twice only did I sleep for two hours without waking (once after the storm and once after coming out of the ITCZ). Normally, each time I woke I would lie in my berth feeling *Fathom's* rhythm before getting up briefly to fill the log, check our position and poke my head topsides for a quick look around the horizon. It seemed enough and I never had trouble getting back to sleep.

Strangely, I never slept during the day regardless of how disturbed the previous night had been. On a couple of nights I had no more than two hours' sleep in total taken in short catnaps. When I finally decided to get up (always pre-dawn) it did take me a short while to feel semi-human but being alone forced me to concentrate positively on what needed to be done for the coming day. I then had to do it as no-one else was around. The only time this initial focus slipped was after 36 hours in the ITCZ and was interestingly at the end of a difficult day rather than first thing in the morning and was, I am sure, due to plain exhaustion. For the rest of the trip I never found myself counting down to my arrival or wanting the trip to finish. I do believe, however, that on a crewed boat my moods would have been less positive. Accommodating others' space, smells and foibles within the confines of a watch system and limited personal legroom when tired would require a different mental approach. It is often underestimated by skippers and crew members planning open water sailing. Personally, I don't think I would be very good at it.

Provisioning

As important as managing my sleep (as far as I could) was the importance of managing what I ate and drank. I started the transat at 15½ stone and ended 23 days later at 15 stone. For the first couple of days the adrenalin, ribs and conditions robbed me of much appetite. However, after that I ate well and remember my first proper supper some 60 hours after leaving and the immediate effect it had on me. It was wonderful and instantly restorative. Thai green curries have now become a standard dish afloat irrespective of where we are. Food had a considerable effect upon my metabolism and mood and although I laughed at Shaunagh's fantastic menu planning (we were still eating tins of tuna, tomato and sweet corn that *Fathom* had carried on the full Atlantic circuit a year later at home in Spain) there is no doubt that part of my enjoyment came from good eating.

In the appendix I have listed the provisioning list for my father in 1963 and my own for 2005. Of the two I have no doubts as to which is preferable. Whilst I never discussed it with him before he died, I imagine his daily menu must have become repetitive and rice-based for much of his trip. Yeuk! With modern technology enabling on-board cooler boxes and/or fridges, supplies of fresh meat, dairy produce and vegetables have become easy ingredients for the long-distance cruising menu.

For those who notice that my father listed a Luger pistol and a .22 rifle as part of his provisioning I am glad to say he never once had to use either – to provide food or repel pirates. I accept that, in extreme cases of shipwreck, a firearm could be useful to secure food. However, for personal protection I see no point in carrying a firearm unless prepared to use it. Even though followed myself, I see little point in waving one at a threatening boat as, in most cases, the occupants are likely to wave (at the very least) something far larger and more lethal back. I doubt I would ever be prepared to use a gun myself and so would never carry one. Even though the world is becoming increasingly dangerous for those who sail in certain parts of the world the dangers seem too uncertain as the tragic death of Sir Peter Blake showed.

Safety features

Happily I never had to use my EPIRBs or liferaft. Likewise, the fire extinguishers and fire blanket remained untouched as did the wooden plugs tied to each stop-cock and the laser torches. Horseshoe lifebuoys, Danbuoys and floating emergency lights all looked good in their holders in the cockpit but realistically, being solo, they would have stayed that way if I had ever gone over the side. However, there is no doubt that all the kit created a sense of reassurance when the weather roughed up.

I have already commented on the usefulness of three reefing points in the main and the removable inner forestay. Both, I would argue, were almost essential and I would certainly fit both in future on any other boat. I also fitted netting on the bows from the stem head to the second stanchion on both sides. Mentally, when working on the foredeck, I felt psychologically more secure and it did allow me to lower the chute easily onto the foredeck without worrying about any part falling overboard and trailing under the keel. In the cockpit I fitted four fold-flat D-rings for my safety lines, one at the top of the companionway, two either side of the cockpit and one at the helm. That way I clipped on before leaving the safety of the saloon and then transferred the safety line to whichever position in the cockpit I wanted.

The one safety feature that I have never seen mentioned but would strongly urge, especially for solo sailors, is fitting a rope along either side of the deck secured at each cleat and with sufficient slack to be pulled over the side in the event of man overboard. I cannot see how any soloist could rely purely on a lifeline and jackstay combination. They would remain attached to the boat but unable to climb back on board without taking the huge gamble of unclipping first. The one safety feature I would happily replace is the webbing jackstays. The endless trips to and from the foredeck were made explosively painful when the metal clasp on my lifeline jammed on the webbing jackstay halfway up the side deck. I would now always have plastic coated wire jackstays even if they need replacing more often. More than anything else, it would have stopped me stupidly unclipping on the side deck on the few occasions I did out of pure frustration and pain.

Agreed plan of action if things went wrong

Whilst I carried the Iridium phone and had agreed to call Shaunagh twice a day I was always worried that something would happen to the phone and I would be unable to call her. Like any piece of electrical equipment in an exposed and salty atmosphere it is not foolproof. Had I stopped transmitting, Shaunagh would have had a bad time. Because of this I had not originally intended to have any radio contact for the whole trip. I had also wondered whether having contact would, in some way, not make me feel far more remote and isolated than maintaining silence. In the end I was glad I took it.

As it was Shaunagh and I discussed and agreed a number of alternative scenarios from a simple broken Iridium to having to abandon ship. In each case we agreed an initial plan of action for both of us. Certain assumptions were made as to whether I was in one piece, the boat was in one piece, the degree of danger and my location. Most agreed actions centred on use of the Iridium or, copying Tony Bullimore, using the small and large EPIRBs as crude communication devices by switching one or the other (depending upon circumstances) on and off rather than leaving them to transmit non-stop automatically. This would also double the effective life of their internal batteries.

Happily such circumstances never arose. I was secretly quite convinced that both of us would completely forget to follow any plan in the event of a misfortune anyway. When things go wrong on a boat they tend to go wrong unexpectedly quickly and the best I could do was prepare the grab bag and keep it at the bottom of the companionway throughout the trip. However, all the emergency pre-planning helped both of us work through most eventualities and having plans for most helped us address the risks of a solo crossing.

Make it fun

In and amongst all the exhausting aspects of preparing the boat, all the sweat of the physical training, the mental logistics and expense of provisioning, the frustrations of co-ordinating delivery/return crews and air tickets and then dealing with all the emotional issues was the small but absolutely vital aspect of making the trip fun. Why undertake such a trip if it wasn't going to be enjoyable?

As far as enjoyable is concerned, I suspect that a solo crossing is not unlike childbirth. Most women I have met, immediately after giving birth, swear never, ever, to put themselves through that experience again. However, six months later, on seeing a friend with a new born baby, that same woman will go all funny and say how wonderful it would be to have another baby as soon as possible. I did not finish with that same feeling of initial 'never again'. I certainly did not feel like Steve Redgrave who, interviewed live on television by the BBC immediately after winning his fourth consecutive Olympic rowing gold medal, authorised anyone to shoot him if he was ever seen near a rowing boat again (which, of course, he was as he won his fifth gold medal four years later). Instead, I empathise hugely with the woman six months after giving birth and being prepared to do it all again for the very simple fact – for all the hard work, it has ultimately given me so much pleasure and profound sense of achievement.

THE WIFE

A hundred years ago men ran away to sea. This description is telling, encompassing as it does the element of running away from as well as the romantic lure they were running to.

When Crispin first said he wanted to sail across the Atlantic I said I would go too. Very sweetly he explained that, no, actually he wanted to go on his own. I spent months trying to decide whether he was running away from or running to.

There is no doubt that watching him sail way from the quayside in Las Palmas is up there with the most wretched moments of my life. The lump in my throat made saying goodbye impossible. I turned and walked away using every ounce of will power not to sob audibly. When I did speak my voice was in my boots and I sounded as though I had been smoking Gitanes in a sleazy bar for weeks.

All the way to the airport, along the coast road I could see *Fathom*, looking cheerful and intent. Intent on going far away from me, intent on taking risks. Intent on stuff from which I was excluded, over which I could exercise no control, could offer no help. Crispin just thought that what he was doing was normal. I later commented waspishly that it was amazing what his lack of imagination had allowed him to achieve! At the airport I ordered brandy for my coffee and tried to regain speech. I knew that Crispin would be in range on his mobile for another hour and after that it would be the satellite phone for a few minutes a day, if it worked. I was terrified that the sat phone would distort his voice as it had done on a previous short trip to Sardinia and that he would sound sleepy, almost drunk. I became obsessed with hearing his voice as it is, normal, calm. I rang him and I was the one who couldn't speak. I sobbed endlessly and spoke brusquely and said nothing very illuminating. Crispin says he doesn't remember me crying. All I remember was crying.

Back in the UK, kind, concerned people kept ringing up, 'How are you? Aren't you worried?' Not terribly helpful. Of course I was worried, terribly worried.

I was not worried because I doubted his sailing skills; I was worried because I know what exhaustion and stress do. I had seen him exhausted, in bad weather, blissfully unaware that both ends of his safety harness were clipped to his wet weather jacket and neither to the boat; I had seen him go forward in the wind and the high seas without clipping on because he needed to do something quickly. I knew the force with which you can be hurled across the cabin and the breakages that follow. It was mistakes and misfortune which had me strung out on taut wires.

Crispin is not someone who relishes being on his own for any length of time; an hour or two gardening; an evening on the computer, maybe, but not weeks and weeks of no one. I worried he would find it hard, exacerbated by exhaustion, poor nutrition, lack of sleep and stress. I hated to think of him unhappy, lonely, afraid. This, as it turned out, was something I needn't have been concerned about. He had the odd low moment, but I think that overall he relished being there, on the high seas, alone, away from the beck and call of others, just doing his own thing in his own time.

I understand the irresistible lure of a challenge. For a man who had worked in banking for 30 years, who had concentrated on providing for his family, who had dealt with clients and problems and other peoples' agendas for so much of his life, a break, away, free must be a prize worth taking. For someone who as a young man had rowed at international level, whose physical fitness and strength had given him confidence and the ability to achieve his goals, the long inexorable slide towards middle age must be harder than for most of us. I knew it was something he had to do; I just prayed that it was not me he was running away from.

Of course it didn't start on the quayside: the project had been dominating our lives for over a year. I had tried to stay engaged with the process of kitting out the boat; bit my lip as the expenditure on gizmos and gear mounted. There were times when I cracked and said I did not want to hear another mention of sailing topics, but then Crispin just went mentally AWOL whilst he lived the dream inside his head and made polite but facile conversation to me. In the end it was better to stay with the programme.

Provisioning was my job and having read various solo sailors' accounts of their time at sea I was determined that if he got a fad for one particular kind of food that he wouldn't run out. Food is a vital psychological prop when far away from home and on your own. I went through the nutritional requirements with Jackie, our trainer, and Alexa, a nutritionist. I worked out how many units of carbohydrate and protein would be needed if he was at sea for 30 days. I did menu plans and hoovered up little delicious tins as I went around to add cheer on the high seas. I brought protein shakes and nut bars, Annie made marmalade; I bicycled back from Waitrose laden with Thai green curry sauces.

We drove the car from London to Spain in order to shift the combination of tool kits, food, clothing and assorted stuff which had accumulated. I shopped for tins and staples in Spain. We laid it all out on and around the kitchen tables; there was a mountain. There were 3 different kinds of rice, quinoa, various pulses and lentils, pasta, long life milk, tins of tuna, sardines, salmon and tins and tins of vegetables. Crispin's stepmother, a veteran of such trips, looked at it sadly. 'After three weeks it all tastes of tins,' she said balefully. We stowed it all on board before the boat set off with crew to wait for us in Las Palmas.

I left the fresh food shopping for Las Palmas. We needed fruit and vegetables, vacuum-packed fresh meat, bread, butter, eggs, chocolate. Once there Crispin did not want to shop . . . 'I've got plenty,' he cried as I dragged him off. We tried the market but the logistics of getting it all back to the boat defeated us. We went to Corte Ingles, the large department store and as we stood in line with our two laden trolleys we saw a sign saying that they delivered to the marina. Halleluiah!

The eggs were the problem. Paranoid about letting cockroaches on board Crispin banned all cardboard and had gone online and bought plastic egg boxes. Sadly the Las Palmas hens lay mighty big eggs and every time I transferred 6 into the new plastic boxes and tried to close the lid they all broke. The work surfaces were swimming in broken egg and I was wiping it up with J-cloths and thinking about heat and salmonella. As Crispin was trying to ease me off the boat I was still swabbing work tops with bleach. Finally I left the cloths soaking in the sink in yet more bleach and stowed the remaining unbroken eggs in bubble wrap in a large saucepan. Then Crispin announced that he was leaving and I had to get off.

For the first two weeks the telephone calls defined my life. I went through my days utterly focused on the next call. I ignored the words and listened to the tone of voice. My husband, I discovered, can lie like a trooper and I can't tell. I knew that Tropical Storm Delta had been big and frightening (hell, it killed nine people in the Canaries, of course I knew) but I did not guess that he had broken ribs. He did not tell me for nine months that he had gone forward to bag his mainsail, not realizing that he was not clipped on, and that a big wave had all but washed him over the side whilst he was calmly believing in the safety harness that could not in fact have saved him. When he was followed by possible pirates and went forward to cover his navigation lights, he was again not clipped on.

On the telephone he made every effort to sound normal, but the energy ebbed from his voice. Sometimes he sounded cheerful, sometimes he sounded lonely, but mostly he just sounded tired. Once he was within reach of Barbados and I knew I could go out and retrieve him by motorboat I relaxed.

When he climbed off the boat at the fuelling pontoon in Port St. Charles marina I was there, jumping up and down like a mad thing. I guided him through the customs clearance – sweet officials who clearly knew that solo-sailors were mad and incoherent and were very patient as Crispin struggled to write his name and fill out the (pretty simple) forms. His lips moved forming the letters like a child. He was way past being reasonable or rational. But he was there.

He had grown a beard on the crossing which made him look quite different. He showered and changed (and discovered that my shampoo had leaked over the one pair of clean trousers and two shirts I had brought out with me. Not popular). We had champagne with Mona on her wonderful terrace overlooking the sea and made polite conversation. But he didn't look like him and when we finally climbed into bed I had to ask him to shave the beard off. I felt as though I was in bed with a stranger. Most odd.

So looking back? I think it was brilliant that he did it.

I would worry less if he did it again, but I would rather go with him and not be worrying back at home. It was a tremendous achievement and it gave Crispin a great psychological boost, but at the end of the day he feels that it was nothing out-of-the-ordinary. Meanwhile I still have nightmares about him falling overboard at night, but there you are, that's wives for you!

THE FATHER: LAS PALMAS TO BARBADOS 1963

This extract was written by my father around 1965 and forms the second part of his 'Family Records' (1962 – Tahiti). His transatlantic crossing was in *Heliousa*, a purpose built 39ft ketch by Jimmy Fife in St Monace (Elie) just east of Rothes in Scotland. On *Heliousa* he and my stepmother, Jinty, then went on to cross the Pacific via the Panama canal, the Galapagos and various Pacific islands and atolls (including Beveridge Reef) reaching Brisbane, Australia, in November 1964.

Having taken delivery of *Heliousa* in June and had a shakedown summer cruise from Scotland to Turkey to visit Jinty's mother we returned to Gibraltar in December 1963. A close study of the Admiralty Routing charts gave us to think that for an easy and rapid crossing of the Atlantic we should start from the Canary Islands with the New Year. Before that, the Trade Winds tended to be lighter and inconsistent; later, and we would be both wasting time and leaving ourselves with less time in the Caribbean, from which one should have moved on in theory before the advent of the hurricane season in August.

There were in all four boats spending Christmas at Las Palmas before setting off for the New World. Apart from ourselves, there were a small sailing boat called Totara owned and crewed by a Belgian couple; a medium-sized yacht containing an American couple and their two year old daughter and a Frenchman called Olivier Stern Veyrin with his daughter aged about 18.

Jinty was keen to have a crew member to come with us in case I became incapacitated or fell overboard, and though I was equally keen not to have one, I gave in as Jinty's request was really quite logical and justified. Casting around Las Palmas we eventually found a young American, Richard Carson, who professed to know the sea and who seemed to us reliable.

So, a couple of days after Christmas we set sail, passing round the north of Grand Canary and then heading south-west to reach the 23rd parallel where we knew we would pick up the Trade Winds to carry us westwards. The night after starting we had a freshening breeze from astern with two sails set and as this strengthened, we turned off the engine to conserve fuel. Rolling along under main and mizzen flattened amidships, we bowled along at close to seven knots for some hours. But as the wind strengthened to perhaps force 7 and the seas increased, I began to think that I should reduce sail. Suddenly and unexpectedly we were pooped by a seventh wave. The cockpit was for a moment awash and a small amount of seawater splashed down into the saloon. But it took only a moment to drop the two sails on deck and continue under engine. This incident is worth recording as it was the only time that we had water in the cockpit during all the time that we had *Heliousa*.

The engine and the autopilot were, undoubtedly, the most essential pieces of equipment. During the 4,000 hours that we were under way during the 18 months voyage to Australia we probably did not steer a total of more than four by hand. Indeed for days at a time we touched no control either on the engine or autopilot, the only task apart from eating being to adjust a sheet once or twice a day and to take sights. Under autopilot, *Heliousa* was very capable at looking after herself. This perpetually posed the difficult question of when to keep watch and when to turn in. The odds of meeting another vessel out there in the huge wastes of water are too small to be counted, but there comes a time when approach to shipping lanes or land raises the risk to a point when one has to chose between the chance of being run down, a possibility very hard to estimate, and the certainty that each of us would have to remain awake half the night with every chance of not seeing a light all that time. It is shaming that complacency and sleep usually won. Every night in the ocean we retired to bed at 21.00hrs or so and slept soundly until morning woken only when the rattle of a block warned that a sheet needed hardening or when Waddy, our Burmese cat, dropped a half-eaten carcass of a flying fish onto our faces.

Jinty always accused me of becoming addicted to

fiddling with the wireless on these long crossings and I must plead guilty to this. It gave one something to do, but much more than this it gave one the illusion that one was still in touch with the world. Otherwise one felt like a traveller through space in a rocket without windows. So hour after hour on the long crossings I stood twiddling the dials and driving Jinty to distraction with my affliction. Another habit I fell into was to sit in the cockpit for hours with eyes ranging ceaselessly back and forth along the horizon all round one. One knew one would see nothing, but I suppose that one's subconscious never gave up its belief that one day it would make contact again with the outside world.

Perhaps others enjoy the open ocean; certainly in their written accounts they seem to do so. They tell me of the teeming life of the seas, of the companionship of marine monsters, of the thrall of the deep and of the exhilaration of gales alternating with the idle ease of calms. The last of these came to us rarely and were always welcome. The rest seemed to us a myth. Admittedly, in crossing the Atlantic we were always accompanied by some breed or another of Mother Carey's hen house, from time to time by dolphins, and thrice by 30ft-long Lesser Rorquals that swam alongside us for hours and once broached clear of the water across our bows, but for most of the time, and particularly in the Pacific, the ocean was barren and bare, boasting but formless specks of scummy jelly from time to time. So we learnt to endure rather than to enjoy the long ocean voyages but gained added excitement from our landfalls. For on these occasions the odours of damp earth became overpoweringly sweet at a range of four to five miles; a few palms took on the splendour of a Tsarist jewel and the first flowers and butterflies became keys to Paradise.

And so, 23 days after we left Las Palmas we caught the smudge on the horizon that was Barbados and not so long afterwards as we rounded the southern end about a couple of miles out to sea, the land smells assailed us, a tropical earthy smell, intensely strong after a month spent mainly at sea. As the anchor rattled out opposite the Yacht Club and the engine noises died away, a blissful calm and sense of having achieved a goal covered us.

We spent about 10 days there using the facilities of the Yacht Club, rather grudgingly and for lack of knowing any other, as it had as members some of the most unpleasant and blimpish racists I have ever met. Alan Godsal had very kindly offered us the cottage behind his Sandy Lane beachside house to recuperate – we needed the rest.

HELIOUSA

Provisioning list 1963 for Atlantic and Pacific

50lbs Coleman's mashed potato powder
24lbs honey
20lbs tinned butter
20lbs flour
20lbs rice
20lbs sugar
20lbs assorted nuts
10lbs raisins
10lbs dried apricots
10lbs dried figs
10lbs prunes
5lbs vegetable cooking lard
72 tins sardines
48 macvita in 2lb sealed tins
48 large cans orange juice
36 large Carnation condensed milk

24 1lb tins Klim dried milk
24 semolina packets
24 1lb tins Golden Syrup
Dehydrated cabbage
Dried baker's yeast in tins
Fresh vegetables (as available before leaving)
12 Whisky bottles
48 Gin bottles
5,000 Cigarettes
12 Large Amplex chlorophyll tablets
DDT cockroach powder and traps
20 tins fly repellent
24 loo rolls
12 large tubes tooth paste
6 large Vosene shampoo
6 large Brylcream
48 large fairy liquid detergent
20lb drum detergent powder
Moth balls
First Aid box
1 Luger 9mm automatic pistol with 200 rounds
1 telescopic .22 rifle with 500 rounds

FATHOM

Provisioning list 2005

Meat (vacuum packed – bacon, chicken, ham, salami)
Fish (vacuum packed – smoked salmon)
12 tins chick peas
12 tins sweet corn
12 tins peas/beans
12 tins tomato
24 tins tuna
6 tins lentils/sausages
6 tins potatoes
8 tins white asparagus
24 eggs
2lbs flour
Various packets of 'cook-in' sauces
Sprouting beans (lots)
Vegetables (lemons, tomatoes, cucumbers, lettuce,
    peppers)

Fruit (apples, tangerines, bananas)
Garlic
Onions
Pasta/couscous/rice/spaghetti
12 tubes tomato puree
4 biscotti, grissini
4lbs coffee
100 tea bags
2 fruit cakes
2 ltrs olive oil (our own from our house in Spain)
3 flora/butter
2 Hellman's mayo
1 jar marmite (large)
3 jars marmalade/apricot jam
Chocolate (bars)
Nuts
Dried fruit
50 high energy snack bars
30 high energy protein drinks
1 large tin assorted biscuits
6 packets of Oreo biscuits
Salt/pepper
1 hot sauce (Tabasco)
1 bottle soy sauce
1 Colman's English mustard
18 pots yoghurt (greek)
6 ltrs UHT milk
75 ltrs drinking water
24 tins Diet Coke
48 bottles beer

6 bottles white wine

6 bottles red wine

3 ½ bottles champagne

2 bottles brandy

24 gout pills!

12 loo rolls

3 tubes toothpaste

1 Head & Shoulders shampoo

2 bars soap

2 bottles washing up liquid

3 boxes matches (long)

1 clothes washing powder (large)

12 bin liners

2 P20 sun screen

2 hand cream

2 large moisturising cream (hand and face)

24 batteries (AA & larger)

THE DELIVERY CREWS

Outbound: L'Estartit marina to Las Palmas via Gibraltar (1,400nm)

Malcolm Eyles, Paul Kibble and Glyn Davies left L'Estartit Marina on Monday 14th November 2005. They arrived 12 days later later on the evening of Friday 25th November having had bad conditions the entire way bar two days. Departure had been delayed by the need to change the impeller but, immediately on leaving and for the first 36 hours they beat into strong southwesterlies, driving rain and large seas. Malcolm later told me that had they stayed longer in the marina he thought they may not have managed to get out for the next two days. Thereafter conditions improved marginally until through Gibraltar where they hove to some 300 miles south west of the Straits for 12 hours during the night of the 21st in gale force winds accompanied by bad lightening. Glyn told us he had lain awake on his berth most of the night clasping the bolt croppers convinced they would be needed before the night was out. Part of the reason for this was they had noticed the rigging was slack although the Nauticmar agent in L'Estartit had previously confirmed he had just completed a full rigging check the week before departure. Upon arrival the Las Palmas Beneteau agent was asked to examine the rig and confirmed the rig had not been touched. In the absence of a professional rigger, Malcolm, Paul and Glyn manually checked and tightened all shrouds.

Inbound; Port St. Charles marina, Barbados to L'Estartit marina via the Azores and Gibraltar (3,200nm)

Graham Ritchie, Ian Ritchie (brother), Myles Bowen (father in law) and Chris Coles left Barbados after 72 hours of preparation on Friday January 13th bound for St Martyn for a shakedown cruise. They arrived on 20th January to provision for the long leg to the Azores for where they departed on the 24th January. On this leg they experienced strong winds and heavy weather. Some 300 miles south-west of the Azores they too hove to for some 17 hours before making port on 11th February. Poor Ian had suffered sea sickness for the entire leg and decided to fly back from the Azores. The remaining three left for Gibraltar on 14th February where they arrived on 21st February and from where Chris had to fly back for business reasons. Graham and Myles (aged 77!) sailed the final leg to L'Estartit marina arriving on Saturday 25th February. Myles had to leave immediately upon arrival but Graham stayed over with us in Spain for the weekend and we had a chance to celebrate their epic voyage and the safe return of all. *Fathom* looking tired but proud came in for rave reviews.